2DO BEFORE I DIE

2DO
Before I Die

THE
DO-IT-YOURSELF
GUIDE TO THE
REST OF YOUR LIFE

Michael Ogden & Chris Day

Little, Brown and Company
New York • Boston

Little, Brown and Company
Time Warner Book Group
1271 Avenue of the Americas
New York, NY 10020
Visit our Web site at www.twbookmark.com

First Edition: May 2005
ISBN 0-316-10972-X

The authors of *2DO Before I Die* take no responsibility for any failed
business ventures, poor-quality poetry, unsuccessful parachute jumps,
or any similar endeavor undertaken as a consequence of the ideas,
suggestions, or stories represented in this book.

Library of Congress Control Number
2005921489

10 9 8 7 6 5 4 3 2 1

Q-T
Printed in the United States of America

For Victoria and Vicki

CONTENTS

Preface _____ xi

Introducing the 2DO List _____ 1

What's on *YOUR* List? _____ 7

Roots _____ 12
Look up an old friend • Own a boat • Meet my childhood hero • Spend the day with another generation • Find my natural mother • Go skateboarding again • Dig out a childhood treasure • Return to my childhood home • Trace my family roots

Explore _____ 30
See the sunrise at the South Pole • Backpack around India • Live in Italy for a year • Climb Mount Fuji • Write to a pen pal • Explore the neighborhood • Road-trip across the USA • See a rainbow at night • Meditate in a Himalayan cave • Go for a good, long walk • Kayak through the jungle

Experiment _____ 50
Shave my head • Streak naked • Grow a beard • Try a new food • Have my own place • Be eccentric • Have a hobby • Build a stereo for my bike • Wear high heels • Do absolutely nothing

Challenge _____ 66
Take up karate • Parachute from a plane • Free-dive to the bottom of the ocean • Get fit • Run with the bulls • Climb a tree • Break a habit • Travel at the speed of sound • Walk on fire

Give _____ 84
Save a life • Repay my debt to society • Leave money for strangers • Help someone in need • Sponsor a town • Support the underdog • Help save an endangered animal • Work with the homeless • Join a protest march • Mentor a child

Learn _____ 102

Perfect a magic trick • Sing opera • Learn to fly a plane • Learn to dance • Keep bees • Learn Italian • Graduate from college • Cook a meal you've never made before • Find a faith • Play the drums • Learn to swim • Pass on a skill

Express _____ 120

Paint on a large canvas • Perform stand-up comedy • Get a tattoo • Draw a self-portrait • Stage a play • Sing in a band • Give a speech • Open an underground arts club • Make your own clothes • Get published • Record an album

Love _____ 142

Propose • Ask out a total stranger • Fall in love • Share a fantasy • Honeymoon in the Galápagos Islands • Come out of the closet • Throw a surprise party for a friend • Start a family • Give birth • Get married

Work _____ 156

Work from home • Change my career • Be a schoolteacher • Take a new route to work • Run a bed and breakfast • Start a second career in my spare time • Open a restaurant • Quit my job

Legacy _____ 174

Bury treasure • Continue a family tradition • Watch my son grow up • Pass on an heirloom • Plant a tree • Follow in my mom's footsteps • Make a family cookbook • Speak from the grave • Build something that lasts • Start all over again

Do or Die _____ 191

The 2DO List _____ 199

Our Thanks _____ 207

Everything is unique, nothing happens more than once in a lifetime. The physical pleasure which a certain woman gave you at a certain moment, the exquisite dish which you ate on a certain day — you will never meet either again. Nothing is repeated, and everything is unparalleled.

The Goncourt Brothers

You will do foolish things, but do them with enthusiasm.

Colette

Preface

Driving back to San Francisco after seeing our grandfather for the very last time, my younger sister and I found there was a lot to talk about. "Grumps," as we called him, was 91 and he knew — we all did — that his time was running out. And for once, Grumps, the inveterate storyteller, never prone to sentimentality, tried to set the record straight. He spent two hours sharing the highlights, as he saw them, of his life.

A self-proclaimed workaholic, to our surprise he spent only about two minutes discussing his career. For most of that afternoon he spoke of people who had played an important role in his life and of particular moments that had brought him some peace, a laugh, an insight.

He told us of his immigrant parents; of his early days as a writer; and of his first love, whose parents had refused their engagement. He mentioned an award he won for a play he wrote in his 20s, the pride he had in his own son's talents, a trip to China he had undertaken in his 70s, and his deep regret that he wrote less and less with the passing of time. Lots of little events, things he might have spent a single afternoon on fifty years earlier, somehow found their way into his thoughts during these last days.

I hadn't heard half the stories. It made me wonder what *I* would remember when I was in his place. Would the last couple of years even get a mention?

As we headed home and our old car ate up the miles, my sister (24) and I (30) realized that this was the first trip we had taken together since our parents' recent divorce. Grumps's perspective on life had sparked off a thousand thoughts in Margaret and me and we soon began swapping stories of our own.

Just out of college, Margaret was struggling to balance paying her bills with trying to figure out how best to move forward. She confessed that — over a bottle of wine with her good friend Erika — she had recently written down a list of things she wanted to do before she died.

To her everlasting credit, Margaret shared her list with me, and her imaginative and honest choices served to wake me up to some ideas worth considering. "Go ahead, take a look," she said. "It's in the glove compartment."

Scanning her handwritten sheet of goals, I could see reflected in her choices parts of my sister that I knew well, plus a number of surprises. Ranging from the serious to the scandalous, Margaret's list of ambitions, desires, and curiosities was as good a self-portrait as any I'd seen. More than that, you could see that in the process of writing it, she had uncovered some unexpected possibilities.

The next day, I sat down over a coffee with a blank sheet of paper. Without thinking about it too much to start with, I wrote the first thing that came to mind — "photograph the Northern Lights." As I wrote it, almost to my surprise, I realized that it was something I genuinely wanted to do. Over the next few days, as I continued to write my own list, I not only remembered a number of ambitions I had forgotten but also discovered several new things I hoped to do — some of them on my own, others along with friends and family.

When I got stuck for ideas, I was reminded of Grumps's life story and the many *small* things he had remembered. I found I took as much pleasure in writing simple plans for the future such as "build a bookcase for my kids" and "own a dog" as I did in the more ambitious stuff. On my list, too, were things that I knew would be there: things I had always wanted to try but had talked myself out of doing.

Of course, I didn't run out and do them all that day, but seeing those goals naked on the page, next to all the other ideas, somehow made them less imposing. Placing them in a context I hadn't really given much thought to before — that life doesn't go on forever — made my reasons not to at least explore them suddenly seem less persuasive.

I wrote down 76 goals over those next few days. For the first time in months, I knew exactly what I wanted to do, and that simple fact filled me with the enthusiasm I needed to begin pursuing some long-held ambitions. Armed with this list of mine, I began to see time as something to work with, not fight against.

Like most things, *2DO Before I Die* started small. Over beers a couple of months later, my friend Chris and I got talking about the list I had made. Chris had his own take, and out of our conversation this project began to take shape. We were curious to get a sense of what other people felt was genuinely memorable and are grateful that so many chose to share their stories.

This book is not an attempt to provide a "definitive" list of things to do. Its aim is really just to stir up the possibilities, bounce around some ideas, and explore both what's important and what's possible. The hope is that through the questions, suggestions, and true stories that follow, you'll want to join that conversation as well.

M.O.

play a sport in front of a
own a dog Take my family on a
ave a photo exhibition See the Sistine
champion a cause witness
a plane have a baby live in a cav
tell the truth speak another la
hav y head use a false
trek across the
arn   ango take a mud b
ca   in Rio make a frien
fo   e refuse a lucrative
on the basis of p
n   on run for o
la   cord an album give bl
sit t   ke a mov
ru   paint a
it my
tion

Introducing
the 2DO List

Looking back on your life so far, what experiences stand out as the most memorable?

In your own scrapbook of events, people, and places, what stories come to mind? Who plays a part? What moments have stayed with you?

Does your mind cast back to the very beginning, recalling those early years of discovery, or do you skip decades ahead and settle on a particular afternoon that made a difference? Maybe you're most proud of the work you've done, the people you've helped, or the times you spent with your friends and family. Or it might be those mad ambitions you felt compelled to chase even when common sense said you should just stay put.

The memories will likely be a combination of all those elements, along with many more. Some things you think of may even be events that seemed insignificant at the time, but now come sharply into focus. Other experiences, maybe more rare, might remain with you until your dying day; moments you felt absolutely switched on and engaged, where you couldn't imagine being anywhere else in the world.

On reflection, you might recognize missed opportunities more clearly — a phone call you never made, a trip you didn't take, a friend you lost touch with, an idea you never saw through — things you really would like to have acted on if only you could have found the time.

Picking out the highlights isn't always easy. We tend to take our own histories for granted. We might have graduated from high school, learned a language, driven across country, raised kids, auditioned for a play, volunteered for a charity, or any number of a thousand other pursuits, but we often dismiss them when we think of our accomplishments. In the rush to consume life, rather than live it, it's no surprise we sometimes lose sight of what's important to us.

In the pages ahead, you'll find dozens of different takes on the same question — true stories from people of all ages detailing experiences both big and small, funny and serious, that have stood out for them as they look back on their lives. These accounts — selected from among those contributed to the *2DO Before I Die* website — range from the everyday to the once-in-a-lifetime. A number of the stories might describe experiences you have had yourself, while some might provide a spark that leads you to investigate new possibilities.

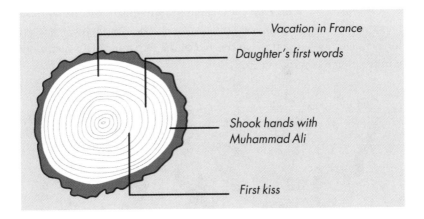

Vacation in France

Daughter's first words

Shook hands with Muhammad Ali

First kiss

We might prefer to put off asking ourselves how life is sizing up until we make it to an older, wrinklier age, surrounded by a family hungry for words of wisdom we've gleaned from a long life. But seeing as we are all going to go one of these days — and given that none of us know when that might be — it's a question worth considering long before that dramatic deathbed scene, if only to confirm we're heading in the right direction.

Imagine yourself then, at the end of your life, compiling a similar list of memorable moments, and reflecting on the things you'll have done up to that point.

What experiences do you hope to have behind you? Will it matter that you never got to hike the Grand Canyon? Is it important you write that novel, even if it never gets published? Given there's only so much time, what would be on your list of things left to do?

When we're surrounded by so many things begging for our attention, it can be hard to see the choices clearly, let alone make decisions as to what's genuinely worth hard work and dedication. From the simplest of everyday pleasures you'd like to make time for, to any lifelong ambitions you're keen to tackle, writing a list of things to do is a chance to remind ourselves of what genuinely captures our curiosity, challenges our imagination, and keeps us involved.

In the back of the book, you'll find a blank 2DO List, with which to record your own ideas as you read through the stories, questions, and suggestions in the following chapters. It's not unlike those "to-do" lists many make to stay on top of daily responsibilities. But while those are likely to end up in the trash at the end of the day, your 2DO List is one you're going to want to keep.

When carving his sculpture of David, the artist Michelangelo famously said he was "releasing" the figure from the marble block — discovering what was already there. Making a 2DO List isn't that different. It's a process of blowing the dust off the document, silencing the static, and exploring ideas that are buried or lounging just on the periphery.

Whether you see yourself as an entrepreneur, adventurer, homemaker, artist, boho, noho, hobo, or no-hoper, there's room for it all when making your list. Consider it your first stab at penning a draft of your sensational memoirs, or a chance to lay out a step-by-step guide toward your chosen career.

It's like an elaborate grocery list. Walk into any store unprepared, and we're immediately faced with a thousand products competing for our interest. If we're hungry, we might grab whatever catches our eye, tossing a deadly combination of doughnuts and frozen pizzas into our shopping cart. If we're well-fed when we arrive, we might just grab a drink and go, only to be pining for food a few hours later. But with a grocery list in hand we have a sense of what we need, not only so we'll have enough to survive on, but also so we might have a few items left to savor. The same goes for the 2DO List.

It doesn't mean we'll be able to afford everything on the shelves, or that all the items on our lists will be available this week or the next, but the chances that we end up empty-handed, starving, or surviving on doughnuts alone become less likely. Limiting the number of options we consider every day can help put our time, money, and energy into things we really are curious to discover. Making the list isn't about accumulating more "stuff" — it's about exploring what's important and weighing our personal needs against a sense of where our responsibilities lie.

There are a lot of lists around these days: Top 10s, top 40s, what's hot, what's not, what's coolish, what's foolish… But the 2DO List is different. Your friends don't write it for you, neither does your partner, child, boss, life coach, or local electrician. In the end it's just you, ready with a pen and this book you're holding.

So consider taking a step back from your everyday life. Ask yourself questions, exchange ideas with friends, and take a fresh look at your life — the past, present, and future. Above all, give yourself the freedom to consider — maybe for the first time — what it is you really want to do with the time you've got left.

Think HUGE

Think tiny

What's on *YOUR* List?

When you're ready to start your 2DO List, here are a few pointers to help you on your way, which can be carefully observed or liberally ignored.

Get comfortable

Whether it helps to go to a café, light a thousand candles, or turn up The Clash on your stereo, it's important to find a space that gives you room to think.

Get equipped

Beyond having a pen and paper, you might also find it helpful to have the following on hand: an atlas, your address book, a calendar, photo albums, your favorite books...

Use the list in the back of the book

From painful, sobering experience, we don't recommend writing anything important on the back of a napkin. In the back of the book you'll find a series of blank spaces in which to record your list.

Be yourself

Be as eccentric, emotional, optimistic, indecent, considerate, nostalgic, or adventurous as you like. The more honest you are the more useful your list will be.

Keep it real

Having X-ray vision, winning a million dollars, or taking a trip to Mars are not without their perks, but it's probably best to bear in mind the bounds of reality when making choices for your list.

Think huge

That said, let yourself come up with ambitious goals, even if you're not sure you're capable of accomplishing them. No need to second-guess yourself just yet.

Think tiny

Sometimes the smaller stuff can be the most surprising of all. There's plenty of room for casual curiosities and everyday experiments on your 2DO List.

Be specific

"Open a restaurant" may not be the full picture if what you really want is to "Open a Naturist mime-themed tapas bar on the western coast of Greece." Try breaking your goals down into as much detail as you can.

A game for one or more players

The choices on your list are yours to make, but swapping ideas with friends can lead to new ideas. Maybe you'll find a few goals you'd like to tackle together.

Write 100 goals

Sounds like a big number, but think of it as writing ten per section. You can stop at ten in total of course (it worked for Moses), but then it's often the last twenty or thirty entries on your list that are the most revealing.

ROOTS ● EXPLORE

LEGACY ●

WORK ●

LOVE

In the pages ahead, you'll be wading through a jungle, trying on high heels, meeting Mr. Rogers, performing stand-up comedy, road-tripping across the USA, throwing yourself out of a plane, joining a protest march, and sharing in the exhaustion and exhilaration of giving birth.

Those are a few of the experiences people wrote about when asked to look back on the events — both big and small — that proved personally memorable and significant.

Together with a series of question games and suggestions of things you could do in a day, these ten chapters aim to inspire choices when considering your own list of things to do.

Where you start is up to you. You may prefer to begin with travel ideas in the "Explore" chapter or look back to your childhood in "Roots." Either way, give your pen a shake, grit your teeth, top up that coffee, and dig deep — you might find some surprises.

No. 1

LOOK UP AN OLD FRIEND

ROOTS

Growing up • Riding your bike • Taking the bus to school • Leaving your shirt untucked • Eating round the family table • Packing your lunch • Staying up past bedtime • Reading comics • Praying for "snow days" • Going on your first date • Earning an allowance • Saving up for a prized possession • Being grounded • Playing ball in the park • Learning to drive • Getting a summer job • Leaving home...

2 Own a boat

Chris, 59, Washington, DC

Driving was not an option. I was only nine years old. Our house perched at the edge of a pond at the end of a long, winding road. My closest friend lived two miles away by land, but only three hundred yards over water. What I wanted more than anything was a boat.

Charlie Casale had just the right one. He owned the tiny Snug Harbor marina with its gas pump, six slips for offshore charter rigs, and eight rental rowboats. He'd been upgrading the rentals to fiberglass and was prepared to unload his last wooden 14-footer for $75.

I had $18.63 in birthday savings and shoeshine proceeds and a pledge from my father to pay me $3.50 to cut and trim the lawn each week. He and I had talked endlessly about the boat and had been together to see it and thump its flat bottom, spending what felt like hours discussing how I might finance the buy. Never had I been so excited as when he offered to go halves and match my $37.50 when I managed to raise it. Charlie agreed to keep the boat until then and kept his word.

For the next three years, the boat was my lifeline to the world beyond our isolated house. The first year I scraped and sanded the hull to bare wood, recaulked seams, repainted it white with red trim, and varnished gunwales. That summer and the next were spent rowing to my friend Alan's house and around the pond, memorizing the location of every rock and poling into shallows to net crabs.

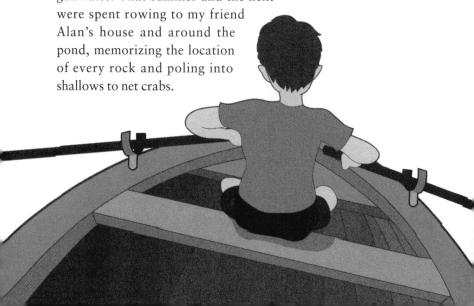

Each year the first weeks of summer were reserved for sanding out scrapes and dings, painting, and varnishing. Around lawn cutting, that is.

My Uncle George, son of a professional sea captain, taught me boat knots. The third summer my Uncle Jim loaned me an ancient, five-horse outboard and I putted hour after hour around the pond and through the channel by Charlie's marina and out past the ocean breakwater to fish for flounder and scup. The engine coughed, burned oil, and regularly threatened to die. That would leave me, I figured, drifting toward Portugal. In fear and anticipation, I brought home from the library Thor Heyerdahl's *Kon-Tiki* to learn how the Norwegian explorer drifted across the Pacific on a balsa log raft.

Late that third summer, and with little warning, Hurricane Carol slashed into New England. Sixty-eight people died. The devastation was enormous. The storm pushed the remains of five houses up on our lawn and ripped my boat from its cinderblock mooring. Frantic and despairing, I looked everywhere but never saw it again. There was no insurance, no replacement. The next summer I went inland, to Scout camp and then away to school.

Before I die, I want to buy another boat.

 ## Meet my childhood hero

Benjamin, 32, New York City

It was the weekend of my 30th birthday, and just a few hours after disembarking the Hyannis ferry. My cell phone was still chattering with business as I stood on the back porch. The last rays of light were spilling over the horizon. New York City was slipping away from me as I settled into the quiet island night.

Suddenly a familiar voice from the edge of the dune asked, "Is the birthday boy here?" I turned to see Mr. Rogers — slighter, perhaps, than I remembered from television, but smiling more broadly than ever — reaching out to shake my hand.

I grew up with him, to be sure. His cardigan and sneakers, though, were mythic. Like Elvis, or John Lennon, Mr. Rogers was an abstrac-

Build a treehouse for my kids · Ride a roller coaster · Host a barbecue

tion — until that late summer evening. See, Mr. Rogers was my neighbor in Madaket, Nantucket. He and his wife, Joanne, summered there in a beautiful clapboard home — The Crooked House, they called it — on Smith's Point. Meeting him that night would change the course of things for me in small but meaningful ways.

The next day, I walked to The Crooked House for lemonade. I was giddy like a little kid as I trudged with my guitar slung over my shoulder through the sandy street toward his home. He answered the back door wearing glasses, a white golf shirt with a sailboat on it, a pair of slacks, and slippers. He was smiling, his eyes like slivers of the brightest, starriest sky you've ever seen. We sat in the living room, there in the back overlooking the sea. It was wood paneled, and strewn with photos and artwork from his television show: there were Lady Elaine, King Friday, and Trolley.

Perhaps the most magical part of my tour occurred in his study, out back behind the garage. There was a desk, a computer, and a small piano, all with a view over the pale green grassy dunes to the silver blue sea. He asked me something no one ever asks. "Tell me about your father," he said. "Your mother doesn't speak about him." And I told him about them divorcing when I was ten, and how it was pretty ugly, and I felt like crying right there on the spot.

That's Mr. Rogers. He asked the hard questions nobody asks. But with more heart than most. And then he said something perfectly appropriate, and real, and substantive, and simple: "That must have been very difficult for you, Benjamin."

Then he rolled his chair over to the piano and began playing. First, he played the theme from his show. "It's a beautiful day in the neighborhood," he sang with a little more swing than on television, smiling. And then he sang "Happy Birthday" to me. Years later, it still seems like a dream.

Outside, Mr. Rogers and I stood on the back porch in the Indian summer sun staring out at the water. He asked me about my job at

MTV. He said he was concerned about modern pop culture. "There is no shortage of things that are shallow and complex," he said. "We need more television, more movies, more art that is deep and simple."

Deep and simple.

The phrase stuck with me. It's what he stood for, who he was. *Mr. Rogers' Neighborhood,* like Mr. Rogers himself, was pure, unadulterated goodness unfettered by extra language, bright colors, or complicated drama. He spoke straight, told the truth, and didn't worry about being cool or contemporary. He just was. Deep and simple.

"I turned to see Mr. Rogers reaching out to shake my hand."

When I returned to Nantucket the following September, I invited Mr. Rogers over for birthday cake. Despite a torrential downpour, and two other commitments elsewhere on the island, he came. He was dressed in a navy blue Carhart jumpsuit, and seemed slower and a bit frailer, but he lit up the room nonetheless. All of us, aged 31 to 56, were transformed into smiling, fawning children.

He sat next to me on the couch, and watched me open a few gifts: a bright yellow T-shirt with King Friday on the front that read "TGIF," and a tiny book with a mirror on the cover and a ribbon bookmark with Trolley on the end of it entitled, "You Are Special." Inside he had written "Happy Birthday, Benjamin! From your neighbor Fred Rogers."

Sitting there with him in the firelight, the storm raging just outside the window, I told him how often I thought about our "deep and simple" conversation, and how often I told others the story. "Spread the message," he said. "Spread the message."

Eulogies are often both hurried and artless. And this is surely both. But it is well intentioned, full of love, and full of gratitude. Gratitude that I had just a moment in the life of one of our time's greatest men. Gratitude that forever more I have a role model who stood for all that is good, honest, sincere, and kind. Now all I have left to do before dying is my absolute best to live a deep and simple life, and spread the message far and wide.

Easy enough, right?

Go paintballing · Have an action figure made of myself · Go rockpooling

SPEND THE DAY

WITH ANOTHER

Perplexed by senior citizens?

Confounded by youth?

GENERATION

no.
4
2 DO DAY

Why not devote your day to bridging the divide between yesteryear and the world of tomorrow?

Go through photo albums and swap stories. Learn of crazy relatives you never got to meet and soak up family fables you might never hear again.

Note: *This is not an excuse for disco-dancing grannies or teenagers playing bingo…*

Find my natural mother

Sharon, 51, Buffalo, NY

A woman had answered when I dialed her phone number that morning. I panicked and hung up without saying a word. Who would I ask for? Who would I say I was? What if she hung up after hearing who was calling? All of these questions and more paralyzed me with fear. I decided it would be harder for her to dismiss me if I showed up at her door, so I arranged for a friend to drive me to her Charlotte, North Carolina, address.

Anxiously, I dressed and undressed, finding I lacked an outfit befitting the occasion. What did a daughter wear to meet her mother for the first time? I settled on paisley culottes and matching vest. Yes, it would have to do.

My friend Don arrived on time and we were on our way. He was excited for me. I was a nervous wreck. An hour or so later, Don pulled his Cadillac in front of a one-story duplex and stopped. The number on the house was 2404. I had the address memorized. I sat in the air-conditioned coolness and practiced my speech. With one hand on the door, I turned to face Don. "Are you sure you'll return in an hour?" I asked. "Yes, I'll be right here," he replied.

I opened the door and waves of heat crumpled the crisp press I had given my outfit before leaving South Carolina. It didn't matter because I had to cross what seemed like blocks before I could reach the porch and knock on the door. There was no bell in sight. "Who is it?" called a voice inside the house. I was silent. The voice called out again, "Who is it?"

"Uh, I'm looking for Mrs. Henrietta McKay."

"Who?"

"Mrs. McKay. Is she here?"

"And who are you?"

"Well ... I'm Sharon, Sharon Richardson, and if you're Henrietta, I'm your daughter."

"Did you say you were Sharon?" She made it sound like Shay-run. And I wanted to run far away at that moment.

"Shay-run, it's really you?"

"Oh my. Come in and let me look at you." I stepped into the cool and dim hall. She closed and locked the door behind me. "Come on in here." I followed her into the living room. A green and gold sofa and loveseat were covered in plastic. She sat down and told me to do the same. I could hear the plastic crunch underneath me as I sat down. She spoke quietly. "I knew you'd come. Yes, I knew you would." Well, I hadn't known I would. My father had convinced me that my mother had abandoned me when I was nine months old. As far as he was concerned, she was dead. I had chosen not to believe the story. I had wanted to believe that somewhere I had a beautiful and loving mother.

At that moment she sat across from me wearing a pair of plaid shorts and a red sleeveless blouse. Her short graying hair was curled and she had a distinctive chin, somewhat pointed. My chin resembled hers.

"Why did you leave me?" I blurted out. This was not what I had rehearsed. I apologized. My mother said she understood. No need for me to be sorry. She was the one who was sorry. I listened as she recalled the details of her departure. It differed greatly from my father's version. I listened intently as she talked. After what seemed like only a few minutes, there was a knock at the door. She went to answer it. Don had returned. An hour had passed. I was surprised and confused. I wanted to hear the rest of the story.

"What did a daughter wear to meet her mother for the first time?"

After I introduced Don, I asked if I could contact her again. Perhaps I could call her? She assured me that would be fine.

I couldn't wait to return to the safety of Don's car. My mother came out on the porch to see us off. I tried to smile as I waved goodbye. As soon as we turned the corner, the tears erupted. Loud sobs followed. I searched frantically in my purse for tissue.

At age 25, I had just met my real mother.

6 Go skateboarding again

Chad, 32, Los Angeles

1988: "Are you sure you want to do that?" I was about to say, as my friend Chris attempted a "boneless" drop-in at our local half-pipe skate ramp. Jumping in the air onto his skateboard, Chris slipped and his face slammed into the concrete with a soft thud as his board flew backwards. We loaded him into a shopping cart, blood trickling from his chin, and headed to the nearest emergency room. Four stitches later, Chris vowed never to return to the half-pipe.

2004: I thought about Chris as I stood outside the "Extreme Skateboard Park" at Chelsea Piers and watched the next generation of skateboarders riding on the state-of-the-art ramps. I scoffed at these youngsters gliding along the smooth Skatelite surface. They had no idea what it was like "back in the day." I watched a teenager perform a picture-perfect boneless drop-in (where one foot is lifted off the board midair while turning around) and my curmudgeonly reverie was replaced with a sense of longing for my own teenage skateboarding days.

I had left my teens behind twelve years ago and had no desire to see them return. But I did miss the skateboarding. Then I remembered that world champion skater Tony Hawk is at least three years older than I am and still skates every day. Perhaps it wasn't too late, after all.

At the skate shop, I was relieved to see a few others who were my age — even a little bit older. Perhaps I wasn't entirely crazy. Then I found out that they were buying skateboards for their kids. So I plunked down $200 for the best skateboard, pads, and XL helmet money could buy.

In order to minimize the number of witnesses to my return to the sport, I showed up minutes after the park opened and headed straight to the "micro-pipe" — the skateboarding equivalent of a kiddies pool. "God bless wrist guards" became my mantra as my muscle memories slowly resurfaced after 16 years of dormancy.

By the time a few 14-year-old skaters arrived at the micro-pipe, I had regained my skating legs, but had yet to "drop-in."

Almost telepathically, a freckle-faced 14-going-on-40-year-old said, "Have you dropped in yet?"

"Not for 16 years."

"Because it's really hard to rock the fakey if you don't drop in."

I was perplexed. "Rock the fakey?"

"Yeah, what you were trying to do."

In the process of moving back and forth along the ramp, I had been trying to "rock the fakey," the same trick I was practicing when Chris split his chin 16 years earlier. It involves locking one set of wheels on the top of the ramp, pausing for a moment, then returning to the bowl without turning around. It's a "fakey" because the skater is pointed opposite their usual direction. It's ramp-riding 101.

The boy had observed my failed attempts silently for about five minutes before saying, "You should really drop in."

"I'm kind of freaked out by it."

The boy smiled. "Oh, yeah, I was scared the first time I did it too."

He proceeded to demonstrate the proper technique with accurate foot placement and weight distribution.

I stood on the edge of the micro-pipe (we're talking a three-foot drop maximum), put my feet into the prescribed position, and hesitated. The boy laughed. "You have to just go for it. The longer you stand there, the more freaked you'll get."

So I pushed my front foot forward and rolled into the middle of the ramp, where I lost my balance and fell backwards.

"You got it. Just lean forward more next time."

So I leaned forward and this time made it across to the other side. I didn't look particularly cool, but I wasn't falling or splitting my chin.

The boy rubbed the chinstrap on his helmet thoughtfully.

"You're ready to rock the fakey now."

"I'm not sure."

The boy-teacher shrugged and said, "You gotta learn sometime."

I dropped in down the ramp, locked my wheel, paused for a single glorious moment, then rolled back into the pipe and fell very, very hard. As a final punctuation to the move, my board flew twenty feet up in the air. After making sure that I had not broken any bones, I felt disheartened. I looked up at the boy, who nodded his head slowly, and smiled. "You got it. You rocked the fakey."

Obviously, there was still a lot of work to do, but the boy was right. It wasn't graceful, but I had rocked the fakey. It's a long way from a boneless drop-in, but, like the kid said, "You gotta learn sometime."

NO. 7

DIG OUT A CHILDHOOD TREASURE

2 DO 2 DAY

Today, dust something off that once meant everything to you and give it pride of place in your living room.

Spend a day reading my old comics - Go to a bowling alley

Return to my childhood home

Page, 37, Washington, DC

A pink Barney Rubble eraser. I know it should be something more Proustian, like a madeleine. But it's the pink eraser that gets to me.

I'm walking through my parents' house in Wilmington, Delaware, the day after they've moved out. It's the house I grew up in and my parents have been here for more than 36 years. With a house and family of my own in Washington, I know I shouldn't keep thinking of this place as my home, but I do.

My childhood home — the stream running behind it where we waded, waged wars, made mud pies; the rusted swing set and seesaw that were finally removed a few years ago; the oak tree towering over the top of the house, its branches sometimes tapping my bedroom window at night, prompting me to leap out of bed, run into my parents' room, and squeeze in next to Mom. When I got too big for their bed, I'd occasionally curl up in the chaise lounge in the corner, somehow comforted by my father's snores.

I come in through the back door and can feel the lump rising in my throat as I enter the kitchen. There's the wooden farm table I'm supposed to take back to Washington, where I live with my husband and two young girls. It seems smaller than I remembered.

"Get a grip," I think to myself. "You're only in the kitchen."

"I know I shouldn't keep thinking of this place as my home, but I do."

I swallow and continue touring the empty house, the one downsizing left behind. Playroom, living room, dining room, den, front hall. Up the stairs I go, passing my old room and heading into Mom and Dad's. The furniture is gone but some stray socks and scarves are scattered across the floor, covered in dust and lint. In the bathroom, there's a curled-up tube of capless toothpaste. "Mom will never learn," I think, looking at the tube. Unlike most children, I was the one who told my mother to put the cap back on.

I decide it's time to venture into my old room.

Now it's empty but for a white wicker rocking chair with a green and white checked cushion. I don't know why the movers left the chair. It's anyone's to take now, I guess. I sit and rock slowly, looking around the room and out the window at the still bare trees of early April. I glance at the wall, remembering how my brother knocked from the other side for predawn Christmas wake-up calls. "Get up, Page. Wake up!" His muffled voice could be heard faintly through the thick plaster.

No longer able to keep my grip, I have a good cry. I cry at the thought of saying goodbye to my house, my room, my childhood. But then I start crying for other things. And my initial soft sobs turn to weeping and, finally, convulsions. I wonder about the future as I sit here, rocking and weeping, in this place of the past.

I notice a swept-up pile of old papers and debris in the corner of the room. Something pink catches my eye. Bending down to pick it up, I realize it's an unused, bubblegum–pink Barney Rubble eraser, the kind we used to put on top of our #2 pencils. It must be more than 25 years old, but it looks brand-new. It's the type of thing once kept in a special box, one filled with foreign coins, a few marbles, a baby tooth, and a Ford–Dole campaign pin. Looking at the eraser, a perfect pink replica of stubby Barney Rubble, I find myself smiling as I hum the *Flintstones* tune.

Okay, now I know I need to get a grip. I know I need to say goodbye, move on. Embrace it and let it go. But it feels like I'm letting go of more than this old house. Here I am at 37 and, for the first time, I feel I'm finally leaving the nest. For good.

Giving the eraser such a tight squeeze it feels like silly putty inside my fist, I waver over whether or not to hurl it back onto the pile of trash. Instead, I put it in my pocket and move on. I imagine my girls will enjoy playing with it when I get home.

Play street hockey · Play softball in the park · Build a robot

Trace my family roots
Peter, 64, Hollister, CA

The postcard-size letters were wedged in a stack about four inches high and bound with beige silk ribbon. On all but two envelopes the stamp had been carefully cut away. The recurring postmark: Nome, Alaska. The dates: June–September 1900.

I was about 10 when I first saw them during a snoop through the cupboards of my paternal grandmother's California apartment. I dared not unwrap them — nor did I ask about them.

Hindsight says: kick myself hard.

Still ribbon-bound, the letters passed to me through inheritance. Yet I failed to read them until I was into my 50s and intrigued with my family's history.

The letters from Charlie, my grandfather, to his wife, Lizzie, tell of his adventures en route to and during what would be the last great American gold rush.

Charlie died before I was born, and any relatives or family friends who might have known of the trip were dead. But the few snippets they had dropped about him while they lived told me he drank, gambled, charmed, flirted, and sang like an angel. All confirmed in the letters to and fro.

> "I was about 10 when I first saw them during a snoop through the cupboards."

Charlie's reportage is rich and vivid and it made me research in depth what went on in Nome during that Golden Summer of 1900.

Charlie tells of the constant daylight, the ceaseless construction work, the people from all ends of the earth drawn to try to discover themselves or find their fortune. Or perhaps just escape.

Those vignettes and what I gleaned from the research drove me to go to Nome in the summer of 1997. I felt compelled to dig for the zeitgeist that on a mid-July day in 1900 had Charlie and more than 20,000 others toiling and spoiling in what today is still the back of beyond — 2,800 miles northwest of San Francisco.

Nome remains last-frontier. And evocative — on the same June day when 96 years earlier the S.S. *St. Paul* rounded Cape Nome, I stood on the beach and in mind's eye watched my grandfather's arrival on a cobalt blue Bering Sea.

I went north into the tundra and glimpsed the environs of Moose Creek, where Charlie had staked claims just before he went home — rich with memories but not gold nuggets. Did he plan to return? Did he want to but could not? If not, why not?

Lately I've been thinking about the odyssey of Charlie's father, my great-grandfather. A journalistic "Johnny Appleseed," he often started up local newspapers where he traveled, leaving vague footprints that one day I'd love to follow.

They trace from Dublin to Liverpool to Melbourne to a town on the west coast of New Zealand's South Island.

Hokitika, here I come...

What place feels most like home?
Name a childhood activity you'd like to do again.
What is your earliest memory? What was your first word?
Name one thing you always wanted as a child, but never received.
What were you scared of when you were a kid?
What was the most memorable family trip you ever took?
Name a member of your extended family you would like to know better.
Do you know where your grandmother was born?
Name a time in your family's history you would like to know more about.
Name one goal your 16-year-old self would have that would not be on your list now.
Is there anything from your childhood you feel you should apologize for?
When did you first feel grown up?

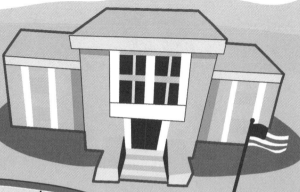

Inspired by a teacher? Helped out by a friend? Name one person from your past you would like to thank.

Was there something you enjoyed doing as a kid, but were advised to leave behind?

Which of your old high school friends would you most like to see again?

What was your favorite book when you were 12?

WHAT'S ON

ROOTS

YOUR LIST?

What would it mean to you now to meet your childhood hero? What would you ask him or her?

What was the most trouble you got into when you were growing up?

NIGHTCLUB

What was the first album you bought with your own money?

Name one thing you wish you had done more of when you were a teenager.

"Explore"

No. 10 SEE THE SUNRISE AT THE SOUTH POLE

EXPLORE

Seeing something with your own eyes
● Swapping stories on a train journey
● Watching new landscapes fly by ●
Tasting unfamiliar foods ● Packing a
snorkel ● Experiencing different cultures ● Breathing in new smells ●
Getting lost ● Learning the words for
beer and *bathroom* ● Ordering squid
when you meant steak ● Writing post-
cards ● Taking photos ● Reaching
your final destination...

11 Backpack around India

Johanna, 32, London

We are often told in the West that we can have anything we desire as long as we want it enough, and strive hard enough for it. The problem is often knowing *what* we want, because our desires are so mediated by all the advertising and marketing we are bombarded with. I knew I wanted something, I just needed to find out what it was. I was ready to quit my stressful job in mental health work and Do Something Else.

To me, buying an open-ended ticket to India and going with absolutely no agenda was a very uncharacteristic, symbolic thing to do. I wanted to strip away all my safety nets and anchors and find out who I was, and what I was capable of.

The usual question people ask me now is, "Didn't you feel unsafe being a single girl traveling alone in an alien country?" The worry in their voices makes me think that I should have been worried after all. But, actually, I had been far too preoccupied with important matters such as whether you could buy guitar strings in India — or indeed string in general — to worry about trivial matters like personal safety.

The night before I left London I had a farewell party and lost my credit card. My dad ordered a new one on my behalf and forwarded it to me at the Post Restante in Rishikesh. Ten days later the card arrived, only to be stolen by a monkey ten minutes later along with a bag of mangos outside the Post Restante. It was another two weeks before a replacement card arrived. I filled up the time with small journeys. When your fate is decided by monkeys you become somewhat humbled.

For me, the key to successful travel in this strange place was to trust my intuition. If I drew you a diagram of my route around northern India during the first three months of my stay it would look something like this:

Hmm, not a very planned, struc- tured, Westernized route to me, I'd say. In fact, the idea of treating my journey like a checklist seemed wrong and stupid. No, I was doing my own

endless, limitless, kamikaze spider of a journey; round and round until I was happy!

I found logic works slightly differently in India and events carried their own kind of magic.

I met a woman at the station in Amritsar who had bought a train ticket to Dehradun (neighboring town to Rishikesh) to do a ten-day silent meditation retreat. I really wanted to do a retreat myself, but I had been procrastinating. She, however, was apprehensive about her trip because she had agreed to meet another girl who had begun to get on her nerves. I had a ticket to the Great Rann of Kutch and the woman seemed very excited about where I was going. At some stage during the conversation my instinctive self, which I had been unknowingly nurturing, decided to take control of events. "OK, let's swap," I said.

So we did it. We swapped tickets, we swapped fates. The woman got on the train to the desert and I got on the train back toward Rishikesh one more time to become silent roommates with the other girl and to do what I had come to India to do: sort out my head. I spent ten long days without speaking, gesturing, writing, reading, or drawing, as I engaged in structured meditation. Temporarily stripping away another layer of "stuff" took me inside to where I could do some much needed mental housework and healing.

For those first three or four months I was very free, but I found out it couldn't last forever. Soon afterward, I settled into a nice, Western, box-ticking kind of route.

In the end, I returned home for a friend's wedding, but I came back a different person. The trip allowed me to become better able to listen to and act on my instincts, which had been so muted pre-India.

Seven years on, I'm still ticking boxes, but with a more certain sense that they are the right ones for me to tick.

12 Live in Italy for a year

Eric, 32, Los Angeles

Almost seven years ago, as newlyweds, my wife and I crawled out of a silver mine in Potosi, Bolivia, skimmed our *Cheapskates and Ramblers Guide to South America*, and almost headed south to find work in Argentina. Instead, we decided to end our trip with the promise that we'd live outside of the United States for a year when we next got the chance.

We returned to Los Angeles just in time for our one-year anniversary, and within six months' time we had full-time careers, car payments, a mortgage, and a first baby on the way. We were living our dream — the American dream — the house, the spouse, the dog, the baby, the yard work, the barbecues, and the big repair projects.

Soon we had our second beautiful child, and as our daughter grew it became hard to imagine ever having enough time or money to live in a foreign country for a year. Then one afternoon, while we were at my mother-in-law's house for lunch, she mentioned how she had just gotten her Italian citizenship back. This meant that my wife and two kids might also become Italian citizens. I looked at my wife holding our baby girl and I looked at our big boy finishing a piece of pie, and all of my dreams of living in another country came together. So I said it: "We should move there. It would be great for the kids to learn some Italian."

My wife loved the idea.

> "We closed our minds to the possibility of failure and charged forward clumsily."

That began the two-year oscillation period where I would go from excited to frightened and back again nearly every day. Questions about logistics overwhelmed me and I found myself doubting the feasibility of going. All of this back and forth tore at my wife. Finally we had a big fight about whose dream it was in the first place. It ended in tears, my wife swearing that she didn't want to go anymore, that I had persuaded her it was just too hard. And she was serious. Part of me had been seeking a way out and had decided it was too difficult. But once I saw clearly what it meant for our dream to be dead, my conviction returned with

See the redwood trees of California - Swim in the Dead Sea - Fish in Tonga

full strength. From that moment, there was no question that we were going.

The question was, how? How was a young couple with two small kids, a big mortgage, no savings, no travel visas, and no clue going to take a year away from their routine to live their dream in Italy? How was it that we were going to be able to pack up our entire lives, find someone to rent our house, and leave? How were we going to get from the point where it was just an idea to where it was a fading memory? Well, we did it the same way we've done everything else in our lives: we closed our minds to the possibility of failure and charged forward clumsily, wrestling with enormous lists of things that needed to get done.

Of course, it meant numerous hours at various Italian police and government agencies, putting up with our children as they chanted, "Who likes Venice? Venice is a nightmare." But it was worth it. To see my five-year-old son play chess with life-size figures in the fog of Lago Maggiore, to see my three-year-old daughter getting her picture taken by tourists from all over the world in St. Mark's Square during Carnevale in Venice, to see my wife snuggle into a towel with our children on the Tyrrhenian Sea while the sun set behind them, to play cards with a man from Naples on the train, to drink grappa with my landlord, to eat seafood at Il Lurido, to walk through the autumn leaves of La Rotunda, to drink homemade wine that smelled like sheep, to have a small Italian basketball coach tell me I was too fat to play, to eat God's gelato, to watch my children climb the ancient steps of their grandfather's first home — for all this, I would have endured a thousand times more nuisance.

There were hidden treasures too — personal discoveries that seemed to be gifted to me for my effort: insight into what it means to be in control, a new sense of the importance of walking and physical activity, an appreciation for not having a job, and, perhaps most important of all, a rekindling of the adventurous love that my wife and I had when first we met so many years ago.

13 Climb Mount Fuji

Eric, 22, Washington, DC

Like the pilgrimage to Mecca, climbing Mount Fuji is something that every Japanese person is supposed to attempt at least once in his lifetime. In fact, the Japanese address Mount Fuji not as an inanimate rock, but by the honorific title of "Fuji-san." Although I am an American, climbing it was a challenge that I had always hoped to attempt.

On the day of the climb, I boarded a bus with a number of my friends at 9 p.m. We reached the mountain at midnight and began to hike. While it might seem strange to begin a journey up a mountain in the dead of night, we were hoping to summit the mountain just as the sun was rising. We were arrogant and cocksure. We had heard stories of Boy Scouts and little old ladies making their way up the face of this tall but gently sloped behemoth, and we were racing each other to the top.

By two in the morning, I already felt exhausted. My friends and I had long since lost each other amidst the hustle and bustle of faces and bodies. There must have been thousands of people climbing the mountain at once, and all that was visible at any time was the ground underfoot, the lights ahead on the trail, and the two people on either side. Every crest brought the hope of the summit, and every ridge simply laid out more and more mountain ahead.

Luckily, the Japanese are quite aware of the draw that Fuji-san holds, and there were numerous huts serving as rest stops along the way. These rest stops are unequaled anywhere in the world; they are totally unrelated to the pit stops on the side of American highways. Each hut was a miniature inn, complete with a full menu, lodging, running water, and full commodes. I stopped in one and, elbow to elbow with an elderly Japanese lady, ate a large bowl of ramen — a nutritious pork-and-noodle soup. Separated from my group though I was, I have never felt such camaraderie as I did in that hut, bridging a generational barrier and a language gap to connect with a total stranger. We discussed the climb ahead and encouraged each other to *ganbatte* — "go for it!" — and reach the top.

By three in the morning — after making quick use of one of the beds in the hut, just to recharge my stores — I was back on the trail.

Within minutes, I passed what could either have been a hairless snow yeti or my friend Joe, fast asleep on a rock. He was in shirtsleeves, was missing his glasses, and had trouble forming coherent sentences, but there was no mistaking it — Joe had passed me on the way up, gone too fast, and had gotten some high-altitude sickness. The two of us pulled it together, egged each other on to get one foot in front of the other, and by first light, we were just below the very top of the mountain.

One of the most welcome sights I have ever seen was the top of Fuji-san at daybreak. Joe was tired, and he could sense that I wanted to reach the top in time more than anything, so he told me to run on ahead. Run I did, and I was so eager to get there that I traversed the loose scree of the face, sprinting up the downhill trail to make my way to the top.

As I watched the sun rise over Fuji-san, I was blown away by the awesome view, payment for the hours of hard hiking. I gazed off of the majestic edge of the mountain and looked down at the country below. It was breathtaking. Out of all of us, only Joe and I had made it all the way to the top. I was pretty proud of myself that day.

Write to a pen pal

Thelma, 71, Woodland Hills, CA

In 1946, when I was thirteen years old, I had open-heart surgery at Boston Children's Hospital. I was there for three weeks. While looking through a magazine one day, I read a story about the International Friendship League. For one dollar they would send me three names of teenagers who wanted to correspond with someone in the U.S.

I started a pen pal friendship with a thirteen-year-old girl named Betty who lived in Yorkshire, England. Our correspondence continued through high school, marriage, the birth of her two boys and my four children.

In 1967, my husband and I took our first trip to England and Betty and I finally met face to face. My husband and I drove from London to Elsecar, the mining town where Betty and her family lived.

When she opened the door of her home, Betty's husband stood back and she and I looked at each other and cried. It was a very emotional scene. We stayed for three days and talked about growing up. I learned that the food and clothing packages I had sent during 1946 kept Betty's family going for many days. Her parents owned a pub in town and her father still kept the ties and sweater I sent them.

Since then, my husband and I have returned five times to Yorkshire, and in 1986 Betty came to the U.S. to stay with my family. We are now both 71 years old and have kept this precious friendship together for nearly 60 years.

I5 EXPLORE
THE NEIGHBORHOOD

Strike back at the subway crush, freeway jams, and irritating lack of inner-city helipads. Today, why not go everywhere under your own steam and take an investigative wander through your neighborhood?

Visit every shop on the main drag – Eavesdrop on other people's conversations – Critique local graffiti – Follow somebody – Act spontaneously – Stroll in the park and savor the feeling of grass beneath your feet

SIGHTS!

Aim high – Look upward at angles you never thought possible.

SMELLS!

Breathe deeply and soak up the fragrances native to your block.

DETAILS!

Take a camera. Snap those signs, spaces, and hidden delights you might otherwise miss.

Walking...

It's what separates us from the monkeys

So, don your most reliable woollen socks, fill your hip flask, and stock up on camera film — the secrets of your neighborhood will soon be revealed...

16   Road-trip across the USA

Andy, 39, Annapolis, MD

There is something quintessentially American about driving across country. I don't know what it is exactly, perhaps it's our history shaped by the journeys westward a century and a half or more ago. Or perhaps it's the movies and their myths of the land and the people. What I do know is that you can't fathom exactly how big America is until you try to drive across it.

What was I hoping to find? I suppose I was too young to understand that I should even be looking for something, much less *finding* something. Back then it was about the experience, the mere going.

And so two friends and I set out of Ann Arbor, Michigan, for the Grand Canyon. We drove. And drove. And drove. Verdant swells of cornfield gave way to arid flatlands. Outside Amarillo, in the Texas panhandle, we got nailed for speeding. I took a picture of the cop. Hours passed. Five. Ten. Twenty. Twenty-four hours later, at 10 p.m., we rolled into Albuquerque, New Mexico. We found the cheapest motel we could, got a room for the three of us, and fell like timber into bed.

After Albuquerque, the landscape began to change and the sky opened up. Cresting a hill, I looked out a hundred miles in any direction. I could see the Earth curve away from me. For that one moment, I understood my small place on the planet. Ego vanished into the distance like the highway ahead.

We stopped occasionally. Petrified forests, rock paintings, and the

ruins of ancient Native homes pierced me. The rock drawings could have been etched the week before.

At last we reached the Grand Canyon. It is, from any angle, magnifi-

Eat sushi in Tokyo - Spend a day in Joshua Tree - Go to Preservation Hall

cent. We favored the less traveled, less trammeled, South Rim. In particular, down in the canyon's belly, I'd recommend seeing the Native American village called Supai.

The stream in Supai comes out of the canyon like a miracle. By the time it surfaces, it is so concentrated with minerals that it is undrinkable, but it is the most radiant blue I have ever seen. Over time, the heavy mineral content creates natural sculptures that resemble petrified water. Long straight veins run lengthwise like muscle fiber. The surface, smooth as ice, appears to ripple, despite its paralysis.

After two days exploring Supai, the three of us headed for its polar opposite: Las Vegas. Life gets bookended where Arizona meets Nevada. The temporal and the permanent, the sacred and the profane coexist here, a mere hour or two's drive from one another. When I come to die, I know that, whether in heaven or hell, the other extreme will be within spitting distance. Each needs the other for comparison.

It being both Sunday and August, Las Vegas was nearly deserted when we arrived. This had its benefits. We booked a cheap room and ended up in a suite with marble fixtures, a nice little bump-up for three dirty kids.

The beer is cheap and plentiful in Vegas, too; free at the higher-stakes tables. We welcomed it eagerly and we gambled a bit. Vegas was everything we'd heard. Cheesy. Awesome. Depressing. Cathartic. Fat lounge singers in bad tuxedos making awful double entendres. Fifty-something couples waddling off buses wearing their best bouffants and bolo ties.

The rest of the trip was spent returning home.

Looking back, I feel I somehow missed it. We spent all our time getting from place to place and none at all along the way. I would like to have taken more time to make the journey, driven more back roads. I would have stopped in truck stops, diners, and roadhouses. I would have met locals — folks who stayed in one place their whole lives. Maybe met people whose dream it was to visit Las Vegas someday. I would have talked to them. I would have liked to hear their story.

I was 23.

Next time, I'll do it right.

Swim in New Zealand · Sail through the islands of Greece · Take a safari

See a rainbow at night

Les, 81, Bristol, UK

These days, when you turn 18 it's common practice to take a year off before continuing with your education. The world is your oyster. The opportunity to explore its wonders is freely available to all, and anywhere can be reached within 24 hours of arriving at your local airport.

Now consider the situation through my eyes — Les, an 18-year-old from the East End of London at the start of the Second World War.

No free will here.

Everyone left school at 14. I was called up by the government to join the British 14th Army, trained in the rudiments of being a soldier, and sent on a troopship for a six-week voyage to fight a Japanese enemy in the remote jungles of a country I had previously never even heard of — Burma.

The monsoon season was in full swing when I arrived, and day after day my colleagues and I hacked our way through the jungle. Usually up to our knees in clinging mud, we forded leech-infested rivers and were constantly wet from top to bottom from the relentless rain, fearful every minute that the enemy would be watching and waiting for us at the next turn.

> "This dire situation was to lead to one of the most extraordinary moments in my life."

Food was in short supply; inevitably dinner meant tins of semiliquid corned beef and dry biscuits, dropped by air when circumstances permitted.

Time became meaningless — no one knew when or how the war would be over or whether in fact we would ever see our homes and families again. And yet this dire situation was to lead to one of the most extraordinary moments in my life.

Having faced some of the worst excesses that Mother Nature could offer, my regiment was withdrawn from Burma to Calcutta so that we could have a rest period and regroup.

One night, with the pressure of battle reduced and the fact that so far I had survived both the terrors of the jungle and the Japanese army, I celebrated with a few bottles of the local brew. Just after midnight it began to rain heavily. In spite of this downpour, a huge silver moon continued to shine brightly.

After a little while, a complete rainbow appeared above us, its vivid colors set against the dark, inky-blue of the Indian night sky. This was something no one in the regiment had ever seen before: a rainbow at night. I was amazed and moved by the sight.

Of course, when I finally returned home to my family, no one believed my story. In fact, it was only after approaching the Meteorological Office more than 50 years later that I was given a written confirmation that such a phenomenon was possible. It was only then everyone finally accepted that my sanity was intact.

Despite the deprivation and utter misery of those three years in the jungle, the experience of seeing the extraordinary beauty of this midnight rainbow — if only for just a few minutes — had a profound effect on me that has lasted to this day.

Whether you are coerced to travel or decide to go under your own steam, one should never be surprised to find the most awe-inspiring sights in the most unlikely of circumstances. Even the horrors of war could not mask the wonders that this planet still holds for us all, and I feel privileged to have witnessed one, albeit in circumstances that I wouldn't want anyone else to endure.

 ## Meditate in a Himalayan cave
Matt, 33, Chicago

Midway through college, I had become stuck. Increasingly dissatisfied with a life that seemed to be happening more *to* me than by me, I had an intense desire to travel far from what I knew. I had grown up in Chicago, and the Himalayas suggested a refuge from the blind and frenetic energy of the big-city America I knew.

So over a three-week period, I walked the Yolmo Valley, nestled in the mountains just north of Kathmandu. Hoping to experience the energy that its many sacred sights were believed to have, my first stop was an 11th-century cave, long used by yogis for meditation. It was missing some of its rustic character thanks to a locking door, a recently poured concrete floor, and a nearby hut for the caretaker, but inside were signs of centuries of religious devotion — worn images of revered saints, statues, butter lamps, and garlands of newly cut flowers — signs of human devotion that hinted at an unseen inner depth.

But sacred places promise more than the basic five senses can offer. As I sat, legs crossed, on a folded mattress pad, wrapped in a sleeping bag, I attempted to settle into the moment. At times my thoughts drifted to home, to my next meal, to the crazy concept of this 20-something American kid meditating in a cave somewhere close to the roof of the world. Even more seductive was the thought of myself actually *being* there. Along with my quest for authentic experience came a desire to envision myself as a mountain hermit-yogi — eschewing society and convention to devote myself fully to the path of spiritual experience. This desire, it turns out, was the biggest impediment of all to my meditation.

In the end, I felt that to view the caves only as destinations was to miss their true power. What I found most valuable wasn't to do with what I found inside them. It was in the inspiration they gave me to explore my own personal space.

So there I was, at 10,000 feet above sea level, a week's walk from the nearest electricity, and on my way to another sacred cave. Crossing over the cloud-covered rim of the valley, I reached a pass marked by stacked stones and a torn prayer flag. Beyond it was a bowl-shaped valley of barren rock, descending to a cliff and overlooking a line of snow-capped peaks that stretched unbroken to the horizon.

Behind me was a plane of clouds stretching, it seemed, across the globe to my home in Chicago. I was literally at the furthest imaginable geographic point from all my family, my friends, and everything to which I was accustomed, yet it felt as though I could reach out and touch them. I had come halfway around the globe on my search for sacred places and found that the most powerful one of all was the one I had brought with me.

19 Go for a good, long walk

Alice, 29, London

The wild, sparsely populated landscape of Glen Coe and Rannoch Moor drew me to walk the West Highland Way in Scotland. There had been a picture of the Highlands on the front of a shortbread biscuit tin we'd had when I was a child, and for years I'd wondered what it actually felt like to be there.

It took me six days to walk The Way, 95 miles of the ancient Scottish pathway. I began the trek at my own pace and with everything I needed — tent and oatcakes mostly — on my back. I was never too far away from concerned fellow walkers offering me high-energy biscuits, high-comfort Band-Aids, high-strength beers, and on one occasion a three-course meal beside a wide iridescent river as the sun went down.

I enjoyed the opportunity to reinvent myself each time I met someone new. I loved the company of people I would never normally encounter who were walking for their own many and varied reasons (to lose seven pounds in a week, to raise money for charity, to train a reluctant rabble of army recruits). But most of all, I loved the hours of solitude and peace as I wound my way around those beautiful hills.

Kayak through the jungle

Hun, 31, New York City

My wife and I left our corporate Manhattan jobs to spend a year in Southeast Asia. On our travels, we took a trip through north-western Laos down to the Thai border that proved particularly memorable for both of us.

There are two ways to make this journey. It can be done in six hours, thirteen passengers huddled in the back of a rusted pickup as it barrels down dusty, winding roads at breakneck speeds. It's a tempting option, despite the jostles. After all, it promises to be the fastest route, dangerous yet exhilarating with its countless blind corners and random water buffalo crossings. Indeed, most locals are rumored to prefer it. But there are others who still speak fondly of the more ancient way.

In a landlocked country such as Laos, rivers have for centuries been the traditional lifelines of the people; they provide sustenance, leisure, and transportation. A river route could also take us in the direction we desired. It would be a much slower path, to be certain, nearly four days before we even reached the fabled Mekong. But we had left New York to see life in its infinite guises. We yearned to feel its pulse, and to listen. So in the end there was no debate. We chose the rivers.

We soon found ourselves deep within the dense green forests of the Nam Ha river, a world where there often seemed to be no sound except the occasional dip of our paddles as we steered absentmindedly along slow stretches. We were lulled into imagining there were no other souls for miles around, though on occasion we would momentarily awaken to see a set of curious eyes peering from between the leaves as a hill tribesman stopped his foraging in the forest and smiled.

There were the villages as well. In the evenings, we found ourselves shivering around open fires while we attempted to communicate with the hospitable locals in Lao, sometimes Thai or English, more often mutual laughter.

One night we drank fermented rice wine from a stone jar with the village chief, and we feasted on roasted rattan and spicy chicken salad atop large banana leaves that served as tablecloth, dish, and decor.

Walk the Silk Road in China - See gorillas in the wild - Watch the Indy 500

Above all, there were the countless smiling faces of the children, eyes aglow with childhood's slippery happiness, when a small activity like writing a Khammu child's name in Korean on scrap paper captivated her and, for us, was a night's finest moment.

We spent three nights on the pristine waterways in northwestern Laos, each day surpassing the one before as we grew accustomed to the river's perpetual cadence. Still, on this fourth and final day, apt words remain elusive. All I know is this: the sun does not pierce the thick morning clouds of the river valley until ten a.m., but the villagers have already awakened at five with the crowing roosters. By five fifteen, through the open-air window of our bamboo-walled room, one hears methodical chopping, a rusty cleaver on wooden block. Chickens squawk for the last time with a shudder of feathers, then blessed silence, and the adults' low chatter mixes with the casual calling of the December rapids.

"We were lulled into imagining that there were no other souls for miles around."

With reluctance, we trade our kayaks for a long-tail boat to carry us down to the Mekong. Along the way, we watch three tiny women balance loaded baskets as they wade waist deep in the cool water without protest or hesitation.

Water buffalo are bound and loaded onto long-tail boats the same as ours, brethren cargo on their way downriver to Houayxai. Children cannot resist waving with both hands to our passing boat while their grandmothers watch with minor amusement and light ornately tooled pipes with an ember from the morning fire. Black stones wrapped in emerald feathers of riverweed lurk beneath this calm surface until the descent forces the water to erupt. Our three boatmen thus draw their bamboo poles and work with quiet brilliance as they navigate seemingly impossible stretches of shallows, and prove nothing is without solution in their able hands.

All of this we have seen today, and only now has the sun made its way down to earth.

If it didn't matter how you got there, what view in all the world would you most like to see with your own eyes?

Name a place you would encourage a friend or a family member to see for themselves.

Name one destination that would appear on your partner's 2DO List.

Is there a sacred place you would like to visit? Jerusalem? Machu Picchu? Graceland?

Of the places you've visited in your life so far, which was the most different from your hometown?

What's the furthest you could travel for $200?

Name one sporting event you'd like to see anywhere in the world.

If you could work abroad for a year, what country would you choose?

Can you name *all* of the U.S. states?

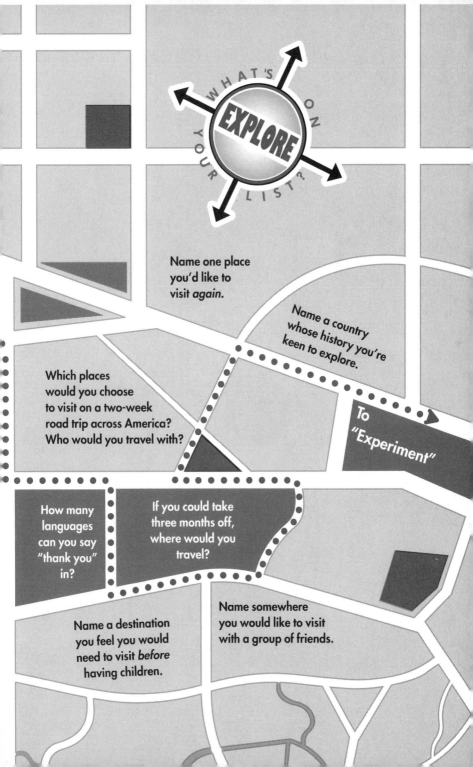

WHAT'S ON YOUR LIST?

EXPLORE

Name one place you'd like to visit *again*.

Name a country whose history you're keen to explore.

Which places would you choose to visit on a two-week road trip across America? Who would you travel with?

To "Experiment"

How many languages can you say "thank you" in?

If you could take three months off, where would you travel?

Name a destination you feel you would need to visit *before* having children.

Name somewhere you would like to visit with a group of friends.

No.21
SHAVE MY HEAD

EXPERIMENT

The exhilaration of trying something new ● Going left instead of right ● Experiencing a sensation for the first time ● Shaking up the routine ● Exploring your boundaries ● Doing something for the hell of it ● Changing how you look just to see how it feels ● Reinventing the way you see the world ● Not worrying what others think ● Satisfying a curiosity ● Surprising yourself...

22 Streak naked

Mandy, 27, Ithaca, NY

I had just graduated from Cornell University a few weeks before and had stayed in town to sing with the Chorus for reunions weekend. Seeing all of the alumni trying to relive their college days made me wonder what I would come back to campus to relive one day. I had never played beer pong. I had never been to a single frat party. I had never gone skinny-dipping in the gorges or had sex with a handsome stranger. I had never done anything even remotely spontaneous. But during a late Saturday afternoon rehearsal of Verdi's *Laudi alla Vergine Maria*, while those thoughts were swimming in my head, the idea came to me: I would streak the Arts Quad that evening.

I don't remember how I convinced and rounded up the other seven Chorus women from my recently graduated class. (Did I pass them notes during rehearsal? Did I just blurt out my secret plan?) However it happened, we agreed to meet at Goldwin Smith Hall ready-to-run at 2 a.m.

I didn't sleep a wink before I got up at 1:45 a.m. and slipped into nothing but my boyfriend's T-shirt (it looked like a dress on me) and my brand-new sneakers. I walked briskly to campus under the cover of darkness and felt more alive than I had felt in months, maybe even years. The chicken in me had picked 2 a.m. because I thought the reunion party might be winding down by then. I was a little surprised to learn that the party was still going strong when I got to the Arts Quad: the tents were still out; people were still dancing and laughing everywhere; and a small group of my co-conspirators had already gathered, most of them deeply drunk from screwing up their courage at a bar in Collegetown.

I was the ringleader and the only sober one, so I mapped out our route. We would run a half-circle around the Arts Quad from statue to statue — from Andrew Dickson White to Ezra Cornell — and we would carry our

Give up TV for a month · Take a mud bath · Redecorate my home

clothes, just in case we got stopped by the campus police. By the time the Clock Tower chimed twice we were ready. I looked around and saw that the group of seven women I had recruited had nearly doubled in size: there were now thirteen of us about to make the run of our lives. I felt dizzy and brave as I shouted for everyone to GO!

It was not a smooth run by any means. Having stripped off my shirt, I had to wait for my friend Gloria after the rest of our group ran off and she struggled to pull her jeans off over her sneakers. The two of us bolted off behind the pack to the sounds of cheers and claps from both young and old alumni alike. I imagined the theme song from *Chariots of Fire* playing somewhere in the night and smiled brightly at my fellow Cornellians as I dodged puddles from the summer rain that evening and the warm breeze caressed my body.

It probably only lasted thirty seconds or so, but I felt like I'd been running forever. I was graceful, lovely, and without breath. I passed the library, the Clock Tower, the flowers, and the Class of 1959 tent. I had intended to only run half a lap, but Gloria realized at Ezra Cornell that she'd left her clothes on the other side, so I joined her on a nude dash back to the starting point. Having never been an athlete in my life, I never knew how fast I could run. Or how it would feel to finally do something impulsive in my 20s.

Grow a beard

Daniel, 37, London

When I was 8 years old, my father grew a beard for an amateur production of *The Yeoman of the Guard*. Then a year later my older brother returned from traveling, also with a full beard — I felt surrounded by old men. Seven years later, before breakfast and without any warning, my father shaved his off, and suddenly I was overjoyed at having a young dad again. Thus began my prejudice against any sort of facial hair.

Beards are for the weak-chinned, I thought, the insecure, the jowly, and the shifty. But sometime last October, I simply crossed a line between sheer laziness in not shaving and growing a beard.

First things first, though. I had a major hurdle to cross: would it grow or would it turn out thin and wispy, in which case it would be out with the razor immediately? To my surprise, it bloody well did grow: thick, multihued, instant ruggedness.

I allowed myself a little male pride at achieving something like manliness after 37 years of being told how young I look; suddenly I felt I'd been admitted to the same psychological society as Ernest Hemingway, Reinhold Messner, Charles Manson — chaps who didn't care about anything other than killing, climbing, and, er...killing. "If the chicks want to tag along, they're welcome, but don't hang on my gun arm." Once this surge of testosterone had ebbed, I started wondering about grooming — a word I had only previously used in relation to horses.

It soon grew to the stage where I was just waiting for that first instance of finding yesterday's dinner in my beard. It was also really starting to itch in a way that was distracting me from important tasks like not scratching while making conversation. So I quietly made my apologies to Hemingway, Messner, et al., and one drunken night took scissors to my chin. In two minutes I transformed myself into one of the Three Musketeers (or perhaps a bloated, blotch-faced Captain Jack Sparrow, for younger readers).

Now it's more of a moustache with a little bit extra beneath the lower lip; selfishly, I love it: it's an organic conversation piece, it keeps my face warm, and if I don't actually look like some of my goateed heroes I certainly feel like them in spirit. What's more, apart from a perverse pride in breaking another taboo (if you thought growing a beard is a loaded act, try wearing a moustache when you're neither gay nor a policeman), I'm now having fun with my face.

I've always been envious of women being able to have their hair "up" or "down" and thus, I imagine, change the way they feel or are perceived in one fell swoop. But now, with aid of a tube of Pinaud Moustache Wax, I can enjoy two distinctive looks: either having my moustache "down" in the style of a 70s German hippie, or "up" and twizzled like a 19th-century satanic goat-abuser's. Either way, it's a win/win situation!! I am, however, planning the "momentous occasion" after which I can shave it all off and lose about 10 years off my face before breakfast.

Buy a painting · Sleep under the stars · Dye my hair a different color

Try a new food

Sarah, 26, New Orleans

For me, as a Southerner, lobster seemed a touch too Yankee to make my 2DO list. If lobster is New England, then crawfish are New Orleans. If lobster is a tiny, two-pronged fork and the appropriate manners, crawfish is sucking the spicy brains out of a mudbug and tossing the carcasses onto the table. Lobster, bourgeois; crawfish, working-class. Eating lobster? A betrayal of my Southern roots. Prohibitively expensive and the stuff of yuppies.

But — as my friend was buying — I thought I ought to try it. It arrived, pink and steaming, looking picturesque with boiled new potatoes and its lemon wedge and parsley garnish, and I announced, proudly, "It's a giant crawfish!" My friend beamed.

"Wait until you taste it," he said. And oh, it was good. Like shrimp, but better. Like amazing-good. Dessert after grandma's cooking-good. First-kiss-good. To my surprise — Yankee food or not — that lobster was as good as it gets.

25 Have my own place

Miriam, 25, New York City

There's a stigma associated with living alone. People wonder about you. They're curious why you don't have a roommate or a significant other with whom you share your space. They suspect that something might be slightly wrong with you. This is not a world for loners. I used to feel this way too, harboring a slight suspicion of those who carried on their lives in a space that belonged only to them. Until I did it myself.

Before I lived alone, but after I made the decision to do it, I worried a lot. I worried that I would be sad coming home to an empty space at the end of the day and about what I would do when something went wrong in the apartment. I worried that I would be lonely. But my living situation had gotten so awful that I had no choice: I couldn't see myself living with another roommate and I didn't have a boyfriend to move in with. So I searched tirelessly, walking into dozens of small, dark, expensive

Ride a scooter - Cross-dress - Invent a cocktail - Go skinny-dipping

places of varying degrees of livability until I found my very own semi-perfect apartment. Before I had even brought the flattened, unpacked boxes down to the garbage room, I knew I had made the right decision. I've never slept more soundly than the first night in that apartment.

Almost immediately, my personality changed. I was no longer burdened with the complications of having another person live in my home: when I was there, I was free to do as I pleased, which in reality consisted mostly of watching extremely bad television, spending an hour in the bathroom with the door open examining my pores, and letting doggie bags from various restaurants pile up in the refrigerator.

Before living on my own, I had always felt like I was on stage, that I needed to keep my flatmate entertained at all times. The relief I felt when I could come home and just be quiet for a few hours was liberating. Suddenly, my best material was ready for social situations and my time at home was my own. Despite the fact that it was extremely small and prone to dustiness, it didn't matter: it was my small home, my dust, and I could do with it all as I pleased.

It also gave me the time to think that I had lacked in my other apartment. All of a sudden, I was writing, I was creating, I was willing to take the chances I hadn't been able to take before, for whatever reason. For me, I needed the whole place to myself in order to create. As soon as I had it, my imagination kicked into gear.

Now I feel badly for everyone who lives with another person. While I do wish that I was in a supportive and loving relationship, I can't imagine having that person in my space at all times. While I do have wonderful friends with whom it might be lovely to go on vacation, I would never again choose to live with one of them. When a friend who has a roommate describes a fight over how one should cut cheddar cheese or whose turn it is to clean the shower, or a coworker describes the relief that she feels when her live-in boyfriend is out of town for the weekend, I can only smile. I don't have to deal with any of that. And while I do think that these people harbor that same suspicion of me that I had of people who lived alone before I did it myself, I also think that they are subconsciously just a little bit jealous.

Live on a houseboat · *Wear cowboy boots* · *Bake my own bread*

Smoke a pipe

An essential prop for savoring the musty odor of a life well lived.

Show no shame

Acts of public nudity, loud and lurid conversation, liberal expletives.

Be ostentatious

An affected laugh, elaborate dress, or exuberantly decorated boudoir.

Insist on something

A lily in your hair, daffodils in your hotel room — make a fuss of such detail.

Dress up

Extravagant headgear & vintage classics to preserve your air of mystery.

Use a false name

A pseudonym, nom de plume, or secret identity to confound all expectations.

Speak in witticisms

Sardonic quips, cunning wordplay & anecdotes to amaze and amuse.

Learn an obscure instrument

Be the sole expert of an unheralded music-maker from another age.

Have a muse

Throw yourself at someone's feet & secure a source of endless poetry.

Drink in a flamboyant fashion

Tinker with absinthe, insist on champagne for breakfast.

no 26 **2DO2DAY**

Be eccentric

Shrug off shame, embarrassment, and fear of cliché — start living life for the memoirs.

Imagine the tales you'll have to tell: singular oddball peculiarities, musty-eyed extravagance, and quick-witted intellectual triumphs.

It all starts today, with your first, sporadic steps into a more extraordinary and decadent world.

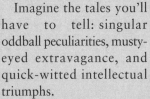

27 Have a hobby
Elizabeth, 29, London

There's an expression my family uses to describe a certain state of being very busy, on your own, just messing around. During these moments, it's not that you're bored, and it's definitely not that you're lazy, but you'd never describe what you were doing as hard work. To anyone else your activities might seem a little pointless, eccentric, maybe downright ridiculous. They might accuse you of being anti-social, of making a mess. Nevertheless you are unmoved by criticism, entirely absorbed, the hours passing like minutes as you are totally committed to fiddling with whatever you are fiddling with. This is the pleasurable practice my family likes to call "bigging and bogging."

I suppose it's just essentially playing, and feeling free to do it, with no expectations, deadlines, or reason, oblivious to other people's judgments. There's always the potential (no guarantees) for something really exciting to come from it. It's harder as you get older, and you have less time and more responsibilities. It can feel self-conscious or selfish to be indulging childish whims, but somehow that makes it more important.

I only realized all of this recently, after college, when I started working in a job, which although well paid, was not particularly creative or stimulating.

I was feeling a bit one-dimensional, like I was forgetting how to use different parts of myself. I thought back to when I was a child and always had a million projects on the go. When one failed or backfired, it hardly registered because I had so many other interests to distract me. I started thinking about the things I had always been drawn to, and how I could reintroduce them into my life. I don't mean I started playing with marbles again, but it's amazing how easy it is to find grown-up versions of the things you enjoyed in childhood.

I joined a trampolining class for adults and also started taking an acrobatics class at a circus skills space. Yes, I look like an idiot, but it's impossible to feel anything but optimistic on a trampoline. Two years ago I decided to take a part-time postgraduate course in photography, and found that the darkroom is a classic arena for bigging and bogging. I made my first pinhole camera out of a cardboard box, spending hours

Try makeup - Regularly ride a bicycle to work - Brew my own beer

experimenting with exposures and light leaks. It was such fantastic escape from my other work, and so perfectly suited my nature, that I never stopped. Last year I had my first solo exhibition of pinhole photography in New York City.

What I really hope now is that one day I can give up the day job and simply big and bog for a living.

Build a stereo for my bike
Andrew, 27, Columbia, SC

I've always loved listening to music in my car. And I've always loved riding my bike. One day, it occurred to me: "I sure would like to listen to music *while* riding my bike." Headphones were not an option. I've never liked wearing them and I thought they would be dangerous as I tooled around Chicago splicing traffic patterns with rhythmic premonition.

So I decided I wanted a stereo that could fit on my bike.

I thought about it for two years, debating methods that would work, wandering in hardware stores looking for that special bolt that would make the plans a reality — all the while fantasizing about how great it would be to hear music while pedaling my bike. I talked about it with people, explained my ideas, but got no advocates for any of my strategies.

Then one day a friend showed me a motorcycle gear catalog that had some several-hundred-dollar leather bag-type thing for holding an AM/FM stereo on the handlebars. In the meantime, I had begun sewing patches and buttons on my clothes, and considered myself an adept sewing aficionado. The lightbulb went on, and I realized I could sew some sort of contraption together and make it work, hopefully.

I bought two miniature, portable, tabletop speakers; I bought the strongest thread I could find; I bought outdoor-grade utility fabric; I bought plastic mesh; I bought Velcro; I bought foam. And I bought a small, removable bag that clipped to the front of the handlebars. I wanted the stereo to be portable, so I could lock my bike up upon arrival at chosen destinations. I spent a few days designing the bag, realizing that access needed to be available to the backs of the speakers so I could change batteries, and generally troubleshooting all the possible dilemmas. Then I spent one day and night making final configurations and sewing it up, listening to the Ramones all night long.

It was solid: the foam was on the handlebars, the Velcro was sewed into the foam, the canvas bag containing the speakers was sewed onto the foam, more Velcro connected the foam to the bag, the batteries were accessible through a flap in the foam, volume on the speakers could be adjusted right in front while riding, the speakers and bag/foam contraption fit into the bag for infinite portability. The only thing missing was a portable stereo. I drove to the store early the next morning, a rainy unbikable day of course, and bought the cheapest tape player they had. I came home, popped it in the bag, plugged it to my speakers, and took it for a test ride. Oh yah. I could feel that funk. The speakers were loose, but the foam was thick — and the sounds were slick.

That was four years ago. They're still pumpin' today, having survived a car crash and a cross-country move. That first summer with the bike stereo I spent at least five days a week cruising Chicago's lakefront — no hands on my bike, no shirt on my chest, a mohawk on my head, and deep dubby echoes coming out of my speakers and into the ears of all the bathers and volleyball players. I thought of myself as The 5-Second DJ, spinning by and bringing sunshine to your ears.

The thrill of listening to music while riding my bike has only grown more intense. I can't imagine any other way to ride.

Investigate a new religion · Be trusted with a secret · Watch the sunrise

29 Wear high heels

Dorothy, 24, Georgetown, DE

Like a bad tattoo or that crazy uncle, being tall is just something you have to live with. There is no way around it. Of course, you always hear, "I would kill to be that tall." This, however, is usually said by a woman who wears a size two and will always be on top if an impromptu chicken fight should arise. But for me, a woman just shy of six feet tall with a bit of substance to her, I find being tall a burden, if just for the lack of footwear.

See, I just could never bring myself to wear heels. Ever. I never saw the need to add extra inches to my already "freakish" height. While shopping for shoes, I would always skip the fashionable section with the stilettos, leopard prints, and hip music and head straight for the "comfortable" department and fight over flats with women double my age. I never wore anything with color or patterns, lest my size-ten feet look like lifeboats from the Carnival Cruise line.

Thus, I stuck with plain, heelless, sensible shoes. I never strayed from the one pair of black or one pair of brown for each season. Why, I figured, when my comfy Easy Spirits would do the trick? Imelda Marcos I am not.

Although I am sure that my shoe collection would fill some 80-year-old female Republican full of envy, whenever I would see my petite, cute girlfriends strut around in shoes I could never dream of wearing, a little pang of sadness would always hit — even when they couldn't walk the two blocks to the next bar because their feet were killing them. In my shoes, I could walk to New Jersey and back and never even get a blister. But, oh, to have my legs look that good! To have thin straps and cute buckles! To wobble unsteadily on my feet! But my fear of being too tall and watching people cock their heads up to glance in my direction was something I couldn't deal with.

Examine something through a microscope - *Organize a treasure hunt*

This all changed when a little piece of mine was selected to be in a New York literary magazine. My feelings of accomplishment and glee were soon replaced with dread and trepidation when I realized I would have to attend the release party, which would be filled with fashionable, beautiful people. My scuffed, drab flats just wouldn't do.

So, with all the strength I could muster, I went to Bloomingdale's to their oh-so-stylish shoe department. Oh, the beauty! There was every kind of uncomfortable and painful-looking shoe on display. I fell head-over-heels in love. Suede shoes! Bows! Bright, bright, bright shoes with polka dots! Purple boots! Platforms! I almost had to sit down and put my head in between my legs to catch my breath. It was podiatry overload.

Ah, but as gorgeous as they all were, how would I, the Amazonian, look in them? I shuddered to think of my towering frame and awkward bearing in three-inch heels no matter how lovely the shoe. After prancing around in various footwear, I finally chose a yellow pair with stripes and a radical (for me) two-inch heel. Their cost was more than my weekly salary. But I was smitten. I now know what Cinderella felt like when she donned the glass slipper.

When the night of the party finally came, I tottered down the street with my new love: my new shoes. I entered, taller than I have ever been in my life, and to my surprise, I looked glamorous and strong. I didn't feel embarrassed or self-conscious — I felt like a million bucks. Hell, I could write, get published, and dunk a basketball, all at the same time.

Okay, sure, they were the most painful things I have ever worn and they only match one outfit, but I will never, ever regret purchasing them (even though I am still to this day paying them off). It's been a year since that party and whereas I still wear my flats most of the time, when I *do* need that extra kick, I will wear my beautiful heels — and a smile.

Live in a commune   -   Grow my own vegetables   -   Go on a blind date

Do absolutely nothing

Nic, 32, New York City

"Carpe Diem." "Sleep when you're dead." "Live every moment like it's your last." OK, yes, fine, I get it. And generally speaking I do it. I live in the city that never sleeps. I have an undergraduate degree from MIT and a graduate degree from Brown. I've produced and directed my own film and published a novel. I visit 6 of the 7 continents with almost pathological regularity. I dive, jump, swim, compete, win, lose, race, race, race. And sex? Well, yes — group, public, foreign, domestic, safe, unsafe, etc., etc., etc....

But when I sat down to write this one, single, solitary page about what I'm really, truly, deeply glad I've done before I die, I realized the one thing that sticks out in my mind — the one thing that isn't a blur — is the day I spent in bed doing absolutely, positively nothing. At all. For no reason. Not even a bad reason. Everything else just kind of blends together, a relentless pursuit of life with only one pause, one moment that I actually stopped, and lay down, and just breathed.

And I can't think of one other thing I've done in my entire life that served as a greater reminder of exactly how lucky I am to be able to do not everything, but anything. A reminder that I can get up and go and do and live. It's not stopping and smelling the roses — even that's doing something. It's doing nothing. We spend so much time achieving, so much time doing — especially in America — that we don't have a moment to consider why we do any of it, why any of it actually matters. Nor do we ever slow down enough to take in the glorious luxury of being able to do what we choose when we choose...even if it's doing nothing. And that's something my day in bed taught me — the importance of looking, of considering, of thinking about what I'm doing and why instead of just doing it. The importance of recognizing how being granted the freedom to do what we want for even just one fleeting instant is a miracle.

Some climb mountains because they're there. I spent a day in bed. And you know what? Now that I think about it, I know what I'll be "doing" tomorrow.

Treat myself to an extravagant lunch - *Invent a board game* to "Challenge"

Name one thing you would not be willing to try.

If you used a false name, what might it be?

Name one thing you've tried that, looking back, you're surprised you did.

Name one thing you'd like to see invented.

Name one ritual you'd like to work into your day.

What is "normal"?

Name an activity you could try that's located between work and home.

Name something you would like to try that would surprise someone you know.

Who in your life has surprised you with the chances they've taken?

Name something impulsive that you could do right now. Who could help you do it?

When was the last time you saw a movie without reading any reviews?

Name one thing that's bad for you but you'd like to try anyway.

Name a food you've never tried that you'd like to taste.

Name one thing you're willing to change about your appearance.

What's on your List?

EXPERIMENT

Name one thing you've persuaded a friend to try.

How long could you keep a vow of silence?

What has been your most embarrassing moment?

Name one totally unfashionable thing you would like to do.

What's the most unusual activity you know a friend of yours has tried?

TAKE UP KARATE

N⁰ 31

CHALLENGE

Putting yourself to the test • Fighting back fears • Risking injury • Feeling your limbs ache • Battling sheer exhaustion • Pushing your endurance to the limit • Feeling your pulse race • Beating your time • Winning a bet • Taking the leap • Scaling heights • Facing danger • Building stamina • Crossing the finishing line • Breathing a sigh of relief...

32 Parachute from a plane

Laurie, 41, Hemet, CA

"Hey, cuz, that's you!" Ted yelled as he rolled down the car windows, pointed at the cloudless blue sky, and drove the rented compact into a dirt parking lot. My olfactory nerves constricted in response to the nauseating stench that emanated from the polluted water of Southern California's not so lovely Lake Elsinore. I held my hand over my mouth and nose, exited the vehicle, and stared in awe just as a dozen or so amoeba-like figures fell from an airplane.

The group soared across the sky like a flock of birds in search of a fine feast. They flipped, twirled, and performed other feats of aerobatics before joining hands and forming a circle in midair. The parachutes released one by one until a man-made rainbow of canvas blanketed the atmosphere above the stinky lake and floated like stray peacock feathers toward the earth.

I turned to my cousin, but he was nowhere in sight. I wandered around the makeshift airfield for a few minutes and headed back to the car. My crafty kinsman reappeared and flashed a ticket in front of my face.

"I bought you a tandem jump," he shouted. "You'll love it! We jump all the time after work."

"Are you nuts?" I wailed. "I don't want to die."

"Look how happy those people are!" Ted motioned to the skydivers returning to solid soil.

I glanced at the wide eyes and ear-to-ear grins plastered on their faces and grimaced. "They're just relieved to have survived."

"Oh, come on." My northern relative poked his lanky finger into my gut. "Since when are you a coward?"

"I don't want to."

"You have to," he explained. "I can't get my money back."

Several cheery voices spoke from a distance: "Go ahead, darlin'!" "It's the best rush in the world." "You'll never be the same again."

"Besides," Ted interjected, "it's a tandem jump. You won't be alone. You'll have an instructor tied to your back. So if you go, he goes with you."

I envisioned broken bones, gooey body fluids, and a closed casket funeral. I sighed, said several prayers, a few four-letter words, and glared at my joyful cousin. My hands trembled as I signed the necessary release of liability forms. I chugged two beers, peed three times, put on the aviation suit, and entered the classroom.

"Strap this belt here, snap this buckle there, and pull this string when I wave my hands in front of you." The instructor's words bounced around my brain like a deflating balloon.

"Pay attention to the altimeter on your chest. If it gets to the yellow zone and I haven't waved my arms in front of you, I've had a heart attack. So by all means pull the string. If that string doesn't release a parachute, pull this string." He tugged on another cord. My heart pounded and I wanted to throw up.

Ted waved as I climbed into the Cessna and prepared for takeoff. No smiling stewardess welcomed me or escorted me to my seat. In fact, there were no seats in the plane, except for the pilot's chair. I plopped my firm butt on the cold metal floorboard and gazed at my fellow sky-divers. I was the only "rookie" on the flight. I looked around and noticed scads of duct tape stuck to various parts of the aircraft's body. I was assured that the plane was safe because the guy who serviced it was a commercial airline captain. The pilot mumbled to someone in the control tower and we were ready for takeoff.

The engine sputtered as it started, the plane squeaked along the path to the runway and struggled off the ground. My heart thundered in my chest and the blood raced through my veins as we reached the 12,000-foot drop zone. The door opened and I shivered in the icy wind as my feet dangled over the edge of the plane. I was certain I was going to die. The instructor told me to cross my arms in front of my chest and jump out on the count of three.

"One... two." I was pushed out of the plane.

Rappel down a cliff · Compete in the Olympics · Drive in a drag race

My face felt as if it had blown through my skull to the back of my head and my body tumbled like a tossed coin. I had no idea which way was up. The instructor tapped my shoulder three times and I raised my arms in the air. My posture straightened, my vision cleared, and I watched the sun set below me. Like an astronaut suspended in space, I felt weightless and separate from the universe. I did not know I was falling faster than 200 feet per second until I looked at the gauge on my chest. Purple mountain peaks appeared and grew tall before my eyes. The instructor waved his hands in front of me and I tugged at the string on the right shoulder strap. The parachute released and opened with a jerking motion that jolted my chin to my chest. I would live!

Acceleration slowed and I felt like I was floating through Heaven's gate. I smiled at the tranquil vastness of the blue Pacific Ocean and observed the silhouettes of Coronado and Catalina Islands.

We appeared to gain momentum and we landed hard on the ground. I lost my footing and squealed with delight as we rolled and tangled in the parachute. We unraveled and I saw my cousin's Cheshire grin.

"That looks like a blast," he said. "I'll have to try it sometime."

Free-dive to the bottom of the ocean
Olly, 29, London

Since reading about pearl divers as a kid, I've wanted to dive as far down as I could swim on a lungful of air and touch the bottom of the ocean. I've been on a couple of scuba dives fifty feet down and loved every moment, but it's not the same. The gear is bulky and breathing out bubbles muffles the stillness of the ocean. Even though I knew there were huge risks, I often wondered what it would feel like to go even deeper, and get there on my own.

About five years ago, in the early spring, I'd hit an all-time low. I was unemployed, penniless, and very single. Although a country boy at heart, I spent my days pacing around a dim, pokey city apartment feeling like a prisoner. The streets outside were packed with busy people rushing for buses and glancing at watches. Unlike me, they all seemed to have a purpose, a job, and a mobile phone.

After a couple of months of this, I was desperate for a change of scene. Though I felt awkward about tagging along at my age, I decided to join my parents on their short summer holiday to Greece.

Soon after arriving, I hired a small rowboat moored at the end of a pier. I took it out to sea a few times and peered over the side. The water was calm, almost peaceful. I thought again about my desire to try free diving. Unsurprisingly, the fear of drowning, blacking out, or having my eardrums burst from the pressure had always been enough to keep me on dry land. But at this particular time in my life the risks were part of the attraction. I needed to prove to myself that I could do something out of the ordinary.

After some prodding, I convinced my father to help me. One still morning, we headed out to sea with a large coil of rope, an anchor, a pair of flippers, and some goggles. We measured out sixty-five feet of rope, attached it to the anchor, and threw it overboard. Maneuvering the boat until the anchor reached the correct depth, I clambered overboard.

The water was freezing. I couldn't see the bottom, just the rope and shafts of light plummeting down into absolute darkness. Seeing my thin, white legs kicking out against the dark blue unsettled me. I spent a few minutes calming myself, slowing down my breathing, before sucking in a load of air and submerging.

I kept my eyes fixed on the rope — it was the only thing to focus on. After about fifteen feet, the temperature of the water dropped. It was cold and getting darker. Thirty feet down and I still couldn't see the bottom. I kept kicking but I felt alone. After a few more hard kicks, the bottom finally loomed toward me, but — anxious and running out of air — I panicked, stopping short of the sandy floor. I just managed to touch the tip of the anchor with my fingers before swiftly turning back to the boat.

Frustrated, I scrambled back on board with my dad. I wanted to conquer that fear I had felt and take the whole experience in. I wanted to touch the sand on the ocean floor.

Become an Eagle Scout · Go hang-gliding · Ride a horse

Confident that this time I could dive deeper, my father and I rowed the boat further out and measured eighty-five feet of rope. I jumped back in the water, took several slow, deep breaths, and dived. As I descended, the rope slid through my hands. My heart was pounding, but I felt calmer and more determined than before.

After a while, I was aware of how still and quiet everything was. Only the deep hum of the sea and the muted sound of a distant boat could be heard. At around fifty feet, distant shapes appeared and the ocean floor again came into view. The last stretch seemed to last forever, sixty feet, seventy feet, eighty feet…But then this time I reached out with my fingers and I was there.

I scooped up a fistful of sand, let it run through my fingers, and took a moment to gaze around. It was strange to be in a place so calm and beautiful, where almost no one goes. The ripples in the seabed stretched into the blue haze. I looked up to the surface in awe of the sheer volume of water above me. The rowing boat was small enough to block out with my thumb.

Several years on, I often think of that moment as a turning point. Completely alone down there, I began to feel like myself again. On those days when the world fails to make much sense, I think of that private place, eighty-five feet below.

2DO2DAY

34. GET FIT

x 20

If you're really serious about doing everything on your list, you'll need to live as long a life as you possibly can.

If nothing else, *2DO Before I Die* does weigh at least a pound, so use it now to extend your life span with a more healthy regime. Lift the book above your head 20 times over the next minute.

Do the same every day until someone asks you what you're doing.

fig A

Survive in the wilderness - Take a vow of silence - Take a yoga class

35 Run with the bulls

Matt, 28, San Diego

Boom! The first cannon sounded and the bulls were unleashed onto the street. I'm not a professional athlete but that cannon did something to me. I felt like I was in "the zone." I realized I needed to keep moving, stay alert, be aware of my surroundings, look around me, notice the faces. I knew I wouldn't be able to see a bull coming, but thought I would be able to tell by the reaction of the crowd where one was. I kept moving, creeping forward, and looking backward. Don't sprint; if I sprint, I thought, I won't be able to look backward.

The goal of the traditional runner is to run alongside the bulls and into the arena with them. This was now second on my list. My immediate goal was to leave Spain without any extra holes in my body. Honestly, if I did not make it into the arena, my ego would still be intact. My legs were weak with fear. If I had any food in my stomach it would have been on the ground. I could cut the tension with the rolled-up newspaper in my hand.

Boom! The second cannon. All six bulls are in the street. People are sprinting by; they just want to make it through alive.

As scared as I am, I can't go with them. I did not come halfway around the world to run in front of the bulls. I want to run *with* the bulls.

I soon lose my brothers in the crowd. We wanted to stick together but it's impossible. We are all like ants scrambling to rebuild our hill after a five-year-old kicks it over. There is little sense to the madness, other than survival. I keep looking back, jumping up to see something, anything. The bulls have to be on their way soon.

Then, out of nowhere, a stout, 2,000-pound beast with razor-sharp horns runs by about ten feet away from me. I couldn't breathe. No warning — there it was. But the bull ran by without noticing me. That was a good thing. One down, five left. Then two more bulls speed by before a third races past me closer. Much closer. I haven't prayed in years and now I find myself praying for safety.

My courage came back in a flash as the last bull ran by. I raised my

Compete in a tournament · Take up rowing · Trek across a desert

paper above my head and ran after the bull like Mel Gibson in *Braveheart.* I stupidly sprinted off after the animal for the last 150 yards heading into the arena, wanting to touch the bull. I didn't think for a second about the bull turning around and goring me — luckily, I didn't have to. My attempt to touch the bull fell short as it ran through the gates. The third cannon rang, letting everyone know the last bull was inside and the streets were once again safe.

I began looking for my two brothers. I found my brother Burke at the meeting point in front of the arena and gave him a bear hug. "My God, we made it!" I belted out. "That was so intense!"

As the arena started to empty we scoured the crowd for the rest of our group. My wonderful wife, Donna, ran up to us, hugged me like a sailor returning from six months at sea, and gave me what I really needed, my bota bag filled with sangria. My younger brother, Scott, and our friend Rigo, both in one piece, found us out front. They had made it all the way into the arena.

After finding everyone, the seven of us headed over to Café Txoko, where everyone goes to exaggerate their war stories of the morning. The walk to the café was a difficult one as the adrenaline drained from my body. I felt good about what I had done, knowing no exaggeration was necessary. It was only 8:30 in the morning and Heinekens were being abundantly consumed. Somewhere between the second and third beer Scott leaned over to me and said, "Let's do it again tomorrow."

36 Climb a tree
Julianne, 34, Los Angeles

I am pushing myself fifty feet up the wobbly rope ladder attached to a sequoia tree in Ojai, California. My clammy palms keep slipping on the rungs. Like the quick throttle of a sewing machine, my legs quake. I want to come down. That's all I want. My fear of heights is paralyzing. Even the automatic task of swallowing takes gargantuan effort. I want to come down.

But I had made a pact with that fourteen-year-old on the ground. Her name is Alisha. She is the quiet one from Compton in my Friday film class. In a mad pairing frenzy typical of teenagers, Alisha was left without a partner for the ropes course activity.

With all the obligatory pep of a high school teacher, I volunteered to be her partner in climbing the tree. It is what any responsible adult would do.

We were to climb fifty feet precisely, in a vertical direction, up the rope ladder to the branch. There at the branch were two wires extending out horizontally, forming the shape of a "V" across the space. The ends of the two wires were fastened, quite securely, to two opposing trees in the distance. We were to slide our way slowly out onto the cables, balancing, as it were, like tightrope walkers. For support, we were to lean out diagonally into empty free-falling space, pressing our palms against each other as we inched sideways. The gap between the cables would gradually grow wider. It was decided that I would scale the ladder first.

Now, dangling twenty-five feet in the air, all I want is to come down. I am not made for heights. I am not cut out for group-bonding exercises. I like dark, brooding satire and Jim Jarmusch movies. Give me a newspaper and a strong cup of coffee any day over this. Anything over this.

The ground is ten zillion miles away. Ten zillion to the tenth power away. Everything seems so...so...vertical. There is only down. Only one direction, down. And I am not going up anymore. No. Up is just not happening.

I'm clinging to the rungs for precious life, wondering if my whimpers are audible on the ground. All I want is my lovely life back and for this to be over. I promise I'll really savor it this time. Be in the Now. Break open that bottle of truffle oil, stuff sprigs of lavender into my pillowcase before bedtime. Floss even.

Alisha is watching with her hands on her hips, composed, expectant. She is not saying anything. Why doesn't she ever say anything?

"Come on, Julianne!" a chorus of students shouts. They are piping out inspirational calendar quotes in regular intervals. "You can do it!"

I wish they would shut up. But I can't rightly yell, "Shut the fuck up!" I can't rightly tell them that up is not an option for me, nor for most of them for that matter. I've seen their test scores.

Cycle the Tour de France · Always take the stairs · Lift weights at the gym

"Release your right hand!" one student advises. "Put it on the next rung up."

They think they know everything, don't they? Well, they don't know everything.

"*I can't!*"

But then there is Alisha on the ground in her plain gray sweatsuit, not saying anything. Just craning her neck, with her hands on her hips, wondering, I suppose, if her partner is a lemon.

Okay, okay. Why should this be so hard? One finger at a time.

The light had a golden hue by the time I pulled myself off the last rung and onto the high wire suspended between the two trees. My legs still quaked while I waited for Alisha to scale the rope ladder to join me. Like a trail horse, she plodded up with wordless resignation. But when she reached the top her eyes were two pleading orbs of fear.

"You're fine," I said, as I tried to talk us both out of the death grip we had on the tree trunk. "We're both fine. There's nothing to be afraid of."

"You sure?" Alisha asked. Her eyes, sharp with fear, were locked on mine as if in search of misgivings.

Why I was asking this child to trust me fifty feet above the earth, fastened to cables of uncertain security, was beyond me. I had no idea what I was doing. I am from the plains of the Midwest. We have no experience with heights.

I reached my hand forward, through the seemingly endlessly gaping space to touch hers.

When Alisha's hand finally released the tree and met mine, everything that once mattered to me dissolved in a wash of color and light. In those minutes, there were no more pieces to publish or industry people to impress, no connections to be made or judgments about what I had done or failed to do. There was only Alisha and I, balanced on the high wire attached to two sequoias — our eyes lucid against a backdrop of soft green leaves and the dappled light.

Hit a home run - *Sail across an ocean* - *Finish something I've started*

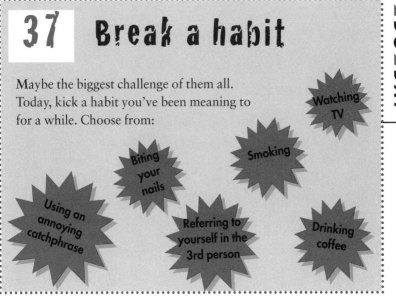

37 Break a habit

Maybe the biggest challenge of them all. Today, kick a habit you've been meaning to for a while. Choose from:

Watching TV

Biting your nails

Smoking

Using an annoying catchphrase

Referring to yourself in the 3rd person

Drinking coffee

38 Travel at the speed of sound

Jim, 65, Santa Fe

The left, logical side of the brain said, "Don't be a dope, fatty, tell them the truth: You are afraid that you will A) crash, B) get blown through the canopy by the ejection seat, C) strangle on your G-suit, D) die of fright, or E) drown in your own vomit because you are too clumsy to take off the oxygen mask when you get sick." That was what the left side of my brain said — the smart side, the side that told me many years ago that I should have become a corporate lawyer instead of a journalist. But the other side of my brain, the right side, the stupid side, the side that told me to become a journalist, and buy a pickup truck and grow a beard, said, "Do it! You only live once! You'll hate yourself forever if you don't."

So this G-suited, harnessed, helmeted, and masked creature somehow climbed into the actual airplane and connected all the hooks, belts,

Stay up for 24 hours straight - Do twenty push-ups every morning

snaps, hoses, and clips, and was ready to go. I was in the rear seat of an F-16B, the two-seat training and qualification version of the Falcon fighter, while Lieutenant Colonel Dordal, the pilot, was in the forward seat. My seat had all the controls and instruments necessary to fly the plane, and all were functioning, although I had been told to use only three of them: the oxygen valve, the microphone switch, and the seat adjustment. There were hundreds of others (including a scary-looking button labeled "nuclear"), but they were not my concern.

Finally, after many checks and calibrations, we taxied out of the hangar and set about flying, which the F-16 did with wonderful élan. Dordal took off by jamming the throttle all the way forward to afterburner. I was slammed back into the seat, we hit 180 knots (about 200 mph) in a few seconds, and up we went with everything intact except my stomach. Then we turned.

Now this needs some explaining. For most of us, the idea of turning in an airplane comes from experiences flying in Boeing 747s and similar aircraft. We know that a turn begins about 20 minutes after a takeoff so gentle you have to look out the window to see whether you're still on the ground. You ask the flight attendant for a gin and tonic and open a copy of the *Herald-Tribune*. You may or may not become aware that the big wing out the window is dipping ever so slightly. That is the kind of turn to which I had become accustomed.

The F-16 turns more promptly. It snaps over to the vertical as quick as a handclap, and before you can yell "Christ Almighty!" you're going back where you came from. Dordal did turns like these a hundred times that afternoon, flipping over and scooting around 90 or 180 degrees as casually as a glance, as if the whole airplane were strapped to him rather than him strapped to it. Look left, go left.

Snap! Bam! Wham!

I looked up at the canopy and couldn't look down again because my head, at maybe 150 pounds, fell back and thudded onto the headrest. My G-suit started to pump up, compressed air rushing through a hose into rubber bladders sewn into the fabric. They squeezed like a boa constrictor, starting with ankles, then calves, then thighs, then, ahem, "waist." There I was, head falling off behind me, fists like andirons, balloons squeezing me to death.

Abruptly, just before I tried to open my mouth far enough to yell "Help!" the F-16 finished the turn and rolled upright. The G-suit deflated and I put my head back up. Good thing too, because I don't know where the vomit would have gone otherwise. The ever-thoughtful "Life Support" team had provided plastic barf bags, stuffed into one of the pockets in the flight suit, and I spewed lunch into it. I had the presence of mind first to unhook the oxygen mask and switch off the microphone so Dordal would not have to hear the sound of a foreign correspondent puking. He politely asked me what I thought of the flight so far. I switched on the microphone and said, "Huunnnngh!" He politely agreed.

But then came an astonishing thing: the peace of flight. High altitude was gentleness and bliss compared with the jinking and dodging on the ground. We went above the clouds to pristine air and bright sunlight. For me, the great moment of the adventure came there, high in the sky, after we joined up to fly in formation. Another F-16 was off to our left, sleek against a background of blinding white clouds. "It's yours, Jim," said Dordal. "I have it, Paul," I replied. I grasped the stick in my right hand, the throttle in my left, and flew the airplane.

I rocked the wings just a little to get the feel of it, and then held the F-16 about 300 feet off the other jet's wingtip as we banked around in a shallow turn. We leveled off and I flew it for a few more minutes, just long enough to sense the power and magic of that pretty, clean, silver airplane, and to gaze at the F-16 alongside us, as if seeing a mirror image. Majestic white cumulonimbus clouds towered up to the east, and I held on to that stick and nursed that throttle and flew that airplane, and at that moment was probably the most placidly, foolishly, aimlessly happy fat man in the world.

One of the Air Force officers had told me earlier that flying an F-16 was the most fun he had ever had with his clothes on. Indeed it was. I would be 50 years old before winter came again, and I don't expect I will ever again do anything as exciting or as sweet or as elegant as fly an F-16.

Not, at least, with my clothes on.

Walk on fire
Sherryl, 35, Madison, AL

The fire walk was held on a crisp November evening in a clearing surrounded by towering pines. A tribal drumbeat pulsed through the air, echoing the beating of my heart. I wanted to walk on fire, but I was afraid. Anxious and excited, but mostly just afraid. The people on either side of me, whose hands I held, reassured me that I was not alone. I was one link in a chain of a hundred, encircling a long coal bed — the fire-walking pit.

In preparation for the fire walk, a husky man smoothed the red-orange coals with a rake. Sparks swarmed like glowing bugs then swirled up on smoke trails into the star-filled sky. The warm scent of the burning wood mingled with the fragrance of pine, the smell reminding me of much safer times.

Earlier in the day we'd written down everything we wanted to rid from our lives. We sacrificed our pieces of paper into the burning coals. Flames devoured my piece of paper, and though my limitations may have been symbolically destroyed, practically, I wondered whether I'd be devoured next. I felt dizzy. What if I fainted and fell onto the coals? Fear whipped my heart into racing full tilt. I stepped back from the pit, paying attention like I was just learning to walk.

"Walk with purpose," our leader said. "Don't stop, but don't hurry either. We wouldn't want anyone to trip and fall." The thought of bursting into flames had been bad enough, but now I possessed a more vivid, excruciatingly painful vision in my mind.

"Focus on your goal," he continued. I wasn't sure whether he was referring to the goal of overcoming our fear or the much more physical goal of the dark green water bucket placed at the far end of the pit.

"Visualize the fire pit as a bed of cool moss." And this would help my roasting feet how, exactly?

I was still waiting for him to tell us the "insiders' knowledge," the trick that would make sense of it all. I had known the fire walk was to be held on the fifth day of this seminar, but I'd always expected to be let in on the secret. He didn't give us any. I was terrified. I couldn't do it. I told myself to leave. But a wiry black man with wild hair began the journey. And I just had to watch.

He strode across the pit, screaming an ancient cry. When he reached the other side, his scream turned triumphant and modern, like that of an exultant winner. I was amazed. Maybe this was possible. I was a safe way back in the line, so I decided to watch and wait.

All too soon, the line before me shrank until I stood at the edge of the fire pit. The radiant heat was intense. I looked down the length and beyond to the water bucket on the other side. It seemed so far away. I didn't think I could do it. This was madness. Close to tears, I reminded myself that I'd just watched many people do it.

Why did I believe they could do it and I couldn't? I got angry with myself. Damned if I wasn't going to walk across that coal bed. Just watch me. I took deep, cleansing breaths until I was calm. I felt a gentle nudge within me and stepped from the cold ground onto the burning coals.

"Cool moss" was my mantra. I didn't feel any heat. I knew I had legs and I knew they were moving, but my mind was apart from my body. Instead, I floated at eye level on a cloud of electric tranquility. It was over too soon. My body pulled me back once my feet plunged into cool water.

Then it hit me — I'd done it! I'd actually walked on fire. If I can do that, I thought to myself, I can do anything.

Go street-jumping - Take a rock-climbing class - Swim the English Channel

What's on
CHALLENGE
Your List?

DOWN	YDS TO GO	QTR
4	15	4

What's the biggest physical risk you've ever taken?

Name one thing you would still like to prove you can do.

When was the last time you were out of breath?

When was the fittest you've ever been?

Name a physically dangerous experience you'd like to try.

Who is your most competitive friend?

Name a sport you would like to play with friends.

Have you ever backed down from doing something at the last minute?

Have you ever been responsible for someone else's safety?

Do you have a sports hero?

2DO

2DO BEFORE I DIE

What words of advice have inspired you?

Name a competition you would like to enter.

Name one exercise you'd like to do daily.

Name a sport you would like to get better at.

Who has been your best coach?

What challenge could you set for your friends?

Name a sport you would like to start playing again.

What song gives you the proverbial "eye of the tiger"?

Name something you would like to train for.

TO "GIVE" …

10

What's the furthest you've ever walked? Swum? Jogged? Biked?

No.40
SAVE A LIFE

GIVE

Putting others first ● Fighting for a cause ● Volunteering your time ● Making sacrifices ● Lending a pair of hands ● Getting involved in the community ● Backing the underdog ● Helping someone through a hard time ● Offering advice ● Standing up for what you believe in ● Staying informed ● Surprising someone with a gift ● Making a donation ● Making a difference...

Repay my debt to society
Paul, 30, Miami

Forgive me, father, for I have sinned. Actually, I'm not a particularly religious person, but I have always tried to lead a morally justifiable existence. Sometimes, though, despite my generally good intentions, I do slip up.

I was seventeen years old and I played guitar in a band. We weren't particularly good, but we did manage to get a couple of gigs playing at a local girls' school. The school in question didn't like the idea of a bunch of guys playing there and pocketing the proceeds themselves, so we were made to play for charity and to charge just 50 cents (!) for tickets. After one of these gigs, I was entrusted with the takings — about $100 — and it was my duty to take it to the nominated charity. This is where my troubles began.

Mostly through my own laziness, the bag of money languished at the bottom of my wardrobe for about a month. Then, one night, I desperately needed some cash for a night out, and — after exhausting all other options — I plundered the charity money. I counted out $20 and left an IOU. Pretty honest of me, I thought.

Perhaps it is needless to say that this happened on a few more occasions and pretty soon I was left with just a few scraps of paper declaring my best intentions to repay the money I had borrowed. OK, stolen. Well, those pieces of paper were accidentally (deliberately) thrown out one day. I knew it was wrong, but the intense spike of guilt I felt back then subsided fairly quickly and I thought no more about it.

Until a few years later at college, when it started to play on my conscience once more. Later still, my guilty conscience grew and grew and my evil, charity-robbing secret gnawed away at me. By this time I was fully employed and could have repaid the money with ease out of the amount I was spending drinking on a Friday night. But still I didn't do the right thing.

Now, obviously, we are not talking about a large amount of money here, but that's not the point. It was the principle of the matter that disturbed me. Stealing from a charity. It's just so despicable.

Give blood · Teach a child to read · Fight crime · Support my family

Then one day I had something of an epiphany. In a newspaper I was reading I saw an appeal from the charity in question — asking for people to make monthly donations. At that moment I was flooded with the most appalling feelings of guilt — years of selfishness finally caught up with me and I completed the form and popped it in the mail.

My relief was not immediate, but I was getting there. I always knew I would have to pay many, many times more back to them than I had taken before I could start to feel better about it. I devised the following formula to help me calculate an appropriate amount to repay:

$$(100 + b)\, c = a$$

Where 100 is the amount I stole, b is ten years interest on that amount, c is equal to "unfathomable guilt," and a is the amount to be repaid. It adds up to a lot.

That was two years ago, and I decided a few months back to increase my monthly "donation" and to keep paying it indefinitely. I am trying not only to clear my encumbrance, but also to make a regular donation on top of that. It really is the least I can do.

In the greater scheme of things maybe none of my actions — good or bad — will amount to much, but as long as I can tip the balance of my own life toward good, I can at least keep a clear conscience and move on with fewer regrets.

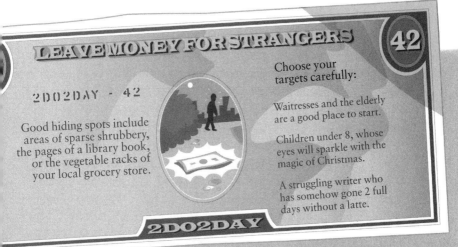

LEAVE MONEY FOR STRANGERS 42

2DO2DAY - 42

Good hiding spots include areas of sparse shrubbery, the pages of a library book, or the vegetable racks of your local grocery store.

Choose your targets carefully:

Waitresses and the elderly are a good place to start.

Children under 8, whose eyes will sparkle with the magic of Christmas.

A struggling writer who has somehow gone 2 full days without a latte.

2DO2DAY

Help someone in need

Celine, 21, Hampshire, UK

For two years I worked and lived as an aide in a children's home in Kwa Zulu Natal, South Africa. When you stay for that long, you naturally form strong bonds with a few of the children and vice versa.

One of these children, a beautiful, intelligent, withdrawn 15-year-old girl named Thulile, came to me and told me she was pregnant. She never said much, words didn't come easily to her, but we spent many days mulling over what would be. Her mother had deserted her, and due to cultural and religious beliefs within the area, she was petrified of being pulled out of school and expelled from the children's home.

Thulile felt that she had committed a terrible "sin." She felt dirty, useless, and guilty for letting people down. Believe it or not, people she respected and looked up to were reinforcing this fear, instead of providing her with the comfort she needed. I remember the midwife who conducted her first pregnancy scan. She looked down at her at said, "You do know that your life is over now, don't you? You've ruined it. It's finished." I was speechless.

"I felt I had to do everything in my power to keep her from sinking further."

I felt very strongly about keeping Thulile safe, even if no one else would. She had become like a younger sister to me and I felt I had to do everything in my power to keep her from sinking further down into that dark place she already felt trapped in.

On her 16th birthday, Thulile was expelled. She was eight months pregnant. She had nowhere to go and I had no authority to convince the management to let her stay. So I got in the truck with her and accompanied her to the valley where she originally came from. Her face was like stone the whole way there. I rested my hand on her back for the entire journey. I felt as if every drop of blood had been drained from my body.

We left Thulile alone, confused, and terrified in an empty house of one of her relatives. All I could do was give her a handful of money and leave my cell phone number scribbled on a piece of paper. I felt nauseous and disgusted with myself for doing nothing more. Later that night I made a conscious decision to fight this at all costs.

Volunteer for the Peace Corps   -   Donate clothes to secondhand shops

The next day I managed to negotiate with my best friend's sister, who lived in a nearby township, to let Thulile stay with her and her family. This was the biggest blessing, for at least Thulile would be safe and cared for. That evening, as I looked after some of the younger children, one of them brought me a note that she found hidden in a drawer. The note was addressed to me. It was, in fact, a suicide note that Thulile had written a couple of months before, when she had swallowed half a bottle of scabies medication.

I had never dreamed she felt that low. I rushed to the management of the home and pleaded with them to do something, but still nobody changed their mind. In their view they were making Thulile an example to the other children: "harming one child to save thousands." I resigned.

I went to Thulile immediately and showed her the note. She felt embarrassed as I questioned her about it, but she reassured me that these feelings had vanished. She knew from that moment that she had no need to feel alone ever again. Things were gradually beginning to look up.

I stayed with her each weekend. We went to every prenatal checkup together, got some decent clothes for the new life about to arrive, made sure she had a good, healthy diet, and waited for the long-awaited day.

At the end of March, at midnight, we rushed to the hospital. By 1:30 p.m. the next day, Thulile had herself a beautiful baby boy. The labor was excruciating for her but Thulile was truly amazing.

The greatest moment for me came when Thulile had just given birth. I placed one hand on her baby, who was now in an incubator, and one on her. Tears flowed down my cheeks as Thulile looked at me and told me the name of her baby boy — Fanele. Translated from Zulu to English, the name means "something that is meant to happen." Every low moment we ever had, every ounce of pain, every injustice vanished.

Thulile is now better and happier than ever. She is still living with the family and has now returned to school to complete her final two years of education. Her son is now one year old and perfect in every way. She adores him, and I know he has a mother with the potential to move mountains.

Recycle my plastics · Save the rain forest · Work as a midwife

44 Sponsor a town

Richard, 38, New Jersey

I read an article in our local paper that featured a town in the northern part of the state that was going through rough times. The businesses were closing down and most of the residents were forced to work several jobs. They couldn't make ends meet. I had never done much charity work and decided to use this as a learning experience for my daughter and her friends who would never see such desperate situations.

We wrote a letter explaining that we were collecting goods to send up to this town. My intentions were to rent a truck and take my daughter and her friends to deliver the items. The response was overwhelming.

We received sweaters, jeans, and jackets that had only been worn once or twice by the teenagers, but would be worn and greatly appreciated by the residents in the neighboring town. The parents of my daughter's friends donated their clothes as well as household items.

I took this opportunity myself to clean out my storage unit, which had been housing old mattresses, bed frames, dining room tables, couches, computers, and bicycles that I had wanted to keep for old times' sake until I finally realized that I should pass them on to these people who could use them today.

> "I decided to use this as a learning experience for my daughter."

I contacted the Chamber of Commerce in this town and let them know what my intentions were. They were thrilled. They arranged with several organizations there to determine what items would be distributed to which groups.

After a week, the items had been delivered. The townspeople took all the goods to their local drive-in and the groups were able to pick up their designated items.

When other people from the town saw what was going on, they asked if they could donate their items as well. The following week they held a sale that raised more than $900, which was distributed to local groups that really needed donations.

Help someone overcome a fear - Open a fair trade coffee shop

45

2DO2DAY

SUPPORT THE UNDERDOG

Today, why not exercise your consumer conscience and give convenience the heave-ho?

Go out of your way to spend your dollars on the mom and pop shops, local artisans, and struggling entrepreneurs in your community. Pick yourself up a nice homemade oven mitt while you're at it...

Help save an endangered animal
Amy, 32, Boston

Going on turtle patrol in Barbados required a full-sized Maglite and several coats of heavy-duty bug repellent. I thought I'd also need a massive dose of caffeine to take me from 8 p.m. to 4 a.m., but I was wrong — good ol' adrenaline did just fine.

So why do turtles need patrolling? As many as five times in six months, a female hawksbill sea turtle will haul herself onto the beach where she was born, choose a nesting site, dig a foot-deep hole, lay up to a hundred and fifty eggs, bury them, and reenter the ocean, never to see her offspring or know their fate. Our mission was to map new nests and to check on previously mapped nests that should have hatched. We unearthed each nest, counted the empty shells, and noted any dead hatchlings — those that had died inside the shell and those that had died after hatching, smothered by sand or of exhaustion.

Of all the hatchlings that did make it out of the nest, every single one could be dead in a matter of days. Disoriented from the artificial lights of surrounding hotels, they might crawl away from the ocean and die of dehydration. If they did find the waves, a variety of ocean predators lurked just offshore. In either direction, seabirds and feral cats waited to pluck their lives away. Only one in a thousand would survive to adulthood — our goal was to improve those odds.

The red phone rang around 2 a.m. A turtle had been spotted on the beach behind a hotel. Patrol to action!

She was magnificent. Watching a turtle on PBS and hearing a soothing British voice explain its activities can't even remotely compare to seeing a two-hundred-pound animal right in front of you, touching its rough, patterned shell, hearing the ocean waves slap the beach just a few yards away. Here was a creature that had likely been born before all our grandparents and might even outlive us. She'd survived miles and miles and years and years of fishing nets, boat propellers, turtle harvesters, sea storms, and many more dangers I couldn't even fathom.

We sat, waited, and watched from a respectful distance as she dug her nest and then faded into her egg-laying trance. Then, we measured her carapace and checked her flipper tag's ID number, which would tell us how often this turtle had returned to this beach and possibly how many nests she'd laid during the season.

After burying her nest, the turtle was surprisingly quick (if a turtle could be quick) to head back down the sloping bank to the ocean. She vanished into the shadowy waves, leaving behind her zigzaggy tracks in the sand, a dozen awed observers, and all her eggs. We marked the nest site on a map, drawing distinctive trees and a nearby stone wall as landmarks. Then, off we went to patrol the remaining hatched nests, our energy renewed by the phenomenon we had just witnessed.

The last nest we uncovered felt like a perfect ending to the night. Three live hatchlings! We placed them gently into a bucket to let them get used to the air, and they scrabbled around, clearly wanting to join their siblings in the ocean. I picked up one hatchling and it fit easily in the palm of my hand. It was so delicate, so light. It didn't seem possible that this fragile creature could survive.

I walked down the bank and set the hatchling near the waterline, leading it to the waves with my flashlight. It moved tentatively at first, then more and more quickly as the ocean called. First it was a turtle, then just a dark speck against the glint of the water on the sand. Then it was gone. I felt sad, but also strangely uplifted. I had given this turtle a few minutes more... or maybe a hundred years more. Perhaps it would be back.

Work with the homeless

Pete, 40, London

Christmas was usually something that I sailed through. But a couple of years ago, I experienced a creeping feeling of nausea brought on by the sheer amount of hard sell that the season can bring. Reuniting with the family for the holidays didn't offer any seasonal cheer either. Emotions ran high that year, and after a whole day of bickering, events culminated in a gigantic, thermonuclear argument. I found myself re-packing my bags, distributing presents like a hungover Santa, and leaving to return to my apartment in the city. For the first time in my entire life I was going to spend Christmas alone.

I remembered a news report I had seen recently that requested help from people with computer skills to work at Crisis at Christmas, a charity involved with homelessness. I thought this might be the oppor-tunity I needed that year — a chance to contribute in a positive way to this "season of goodwill." A few clicks on the Internet and I had volun-teered. I imagined myself helping out at the call center knee deep in cables, but when the instructions came, the reality was somewhat different.

I was required both on Christmas Day and Boxing Day to help at "The Drinkers Shelter," the only hostel in the city that catered to home-less drinkers over the Christmas period.

When I arrived at the center on Christmas Day, the first thing that struck me was the smell. A strange musky miasma, like the ghost of a million garage sales. Undeterred, I made my way to the Helpers' Welcome Center for my induction talk. Within minutes of listening to what we could expect during our shift, I had nothing but admiration for the staff, many of whom were giving up their entire Christmas season to plan and execute what was clearly a gigantic undertaking.

The induction talk was given by Jim, a smiley Scotsman in his early 40s who told me and my fellow volunteers how our help would be most useful to Crisis. First, they needed us to simply talk to the "clients." Apparently there is no substitute for just sitting and talking to people who have, quite often, been ignored for most of their lives. With a few

Donate to a dogs' home - Buy an eco-friendly car - Cook my parents dinner

tips about other ways to help, I put on my name badge and made my way into the shelter.

It was pointed out to me by the staff that homelessness is a problem that when linked with alcohol and drug dependency takes more than just a desire to beat it; it needs professional help. As for the alcohol use itself, I was struck by how it affected each individual differently. Many were loud, humorous, and very touchy-feely. Others were broody and sullen and at times aggressive and violent.

"There is no substitute for just sitting and talking to people."

I really became aware just how debilitating an alcohol addiction can be when I met Taff. Sensing that he was relaxed, I quizzed Taff as to how he had become homeless. He charted a downward spiral of abusive parents before running away to the city. He had been drinking since childhood. The amount he had consumed that day meant that he could not even keep a glass of water in his stomach.

I asked Taff to join me at the large Christmas meal that was being prepared in the canteen. He decided to give it his best shot.

When we entered the dining area, there were still a few territorial issues being settled. Some people steadfastly refused to eat in the same room as others but things eventually became quiet enough for everyone, staff and clients alike, to don Christmas hats and dine together. Of the whole experience, this was the most memorable moment for me, probably because it was a reminder of what Christmas can be — an example of what can be achieved when those who have and who can, get together to help those who have not and who cannot.

Looking back, I was touched by how friendly the rest of the volunteers at the shelter were and by their myriad reasons for being available that Christmas. Similarly, the Crisis staff themselves were heroic figures, extremely grateful for any help and adept at dealing with all kinds of situations and people, often regardless of their own safety. They really were to be admired.

Pick up basic first aid · Swear less often · Collect donations for a charity

48 Join a protest march

Chris, 29, London

My pragmatic, conservative background had taught me that if you felt the need to shout in the street you were either clearly insane or deeply naive. From our safe, comfortable middle-class perspective, there seemed something dangerously uncivilized about the act of protest. Passionate people inspired by injustice to take to the streets were a million miles away from my family's world, where making a fuss at the refunds counter of a department store was the closest you'd ever come to standing up for your rights.

This ingrained view of the world weakened a little when I left home, evolved further over time, and finally collapsed when my country's government declared its intention to invade a country some 3,000 miles away.

I didn't know the war was wrong for sure. The overload of information didn't help — not *all* the arguments really made sense, and part of me was even prepared to trust our leader in his fearful summary of the consequences of inaction. But it still all struck me as deeply fishy, suspiciously convenient, and an unhealthy precedent for the future.

Enough people felt the same way for there to be a march through London planned for the following weekend. When I saw the flyers and watched the news I found myself considering for the first time the idea of taking to the streets and joining in.

I spoke to my sister on the phone a few days before the march was due to take place. I think I was trying to provoke her by announcing my plan to join the protest. She wasn't impressed and, in her wonderfully patronizing way, told me exactly why she trusted those in power and saw the war as the only option.

Her attitude deflated me, but — more importantly — I found that she actually seemed far more informed than I was and confident about her stance. I envied that. I was reacting with my heart to a crazy situation, but how much did I *really* know? Did I have the facts to back up my suspicious instincts? Did I really have the courage of my convictions?

I resolved there and then to join the march — to stop being a bystander and a theorizer and get my hands dirty with the idea of being more politicized.

I was almost more worried about *not* going than going. How would it feel? This tantalizing opportunity to make my voice heard and I didn't have the guts to take my place amongst the crowds? How could I talk about it with conviction in the future if I didn't step up to the plate and join in?

When my wife and I arrived at the spot, my genetic reservations kicked in again. As we ascended the subway stairs to the street, the chanting and general hubbub struck me as intimidating. There was a hint of revolution in the air. Thousands of people had gathered. How could I fit in? How could this seething mass that snaked through the streets possibly represent a single opinion — my opinion?

Awkwardly, we stepped over the barrier that divided us from the crowds. We crept into line and left the ranks of the silent majority.

Once in the crowd I saw a breed of people that broke the TV news stereotype of "the protestor." These weren't rabble-rousers. Not union-ized workers defending their jobs or tie-dyed travelers strapping themselves to trees. This was the first protest for a great many that day. Entire families were there, sensibly clothed, their raincoats packed away in backpacks. Sandwiches were distributed, flasks of hot soup passed round. At times it felt more of a camping trip than an attempt to prevent the next world war.

After various speeches delivered from a temporary stage, it was announced that this was the largest single gathering in the history of the city. Everyone let out a cheer.

As the rally came to a close, my wife and I headed home. A few streets away we found ourselves walking right down the middle of the road. We felt a fresh sense of freedom, that we could walk anywhere, that these streets now somehow belonged to us and our fellow protestors. The experience had left us feeling empowered, as if we had just voted.

Like most people on the march, I knew this day alone wouldn't be enough to *really* stop the war. But I did feel that enough noise was made so that next time those in charge might think again. When that protest comes around, I'd better have a damn good excuse not to be there.

Join the military - *Work in a refugee camp* - *Learn sign language*

49 Mentor a child
Graham, 20, Indianapolis

We met for the first time in a cramped, noisy daycare room. The room smelled like kids: peanut butter and jelly sandwiches, playground dirt, craft glue, and crayons. At nearly six-and-a-half feet tall, I towered above most of the elementary school children and immediately attracted a band of followers, curious about my name, my age, and especially my height.

All these little greeters enthusiastically showed me around their after-school home: the daycare center for the children of residents or former residents of the Rise. The Rise is an intermediate housing facility in Indiana for women and children who are victims of domestic violence.

To the Rise, I am part of their effort to stop the cycle of domestic violence that starts when children are raised in abusive homes. Their belief is that with a positive role model in addition to good parenting, a child can learn good study habits and make healthy lifestyle choices. I had been looking to get more involved in the local community at college and mentoring at the Rise seemed like an excellent opportunity.

After the grand tour from two eight-year-old girls, a daycare worker came and greeted me. I told her my name and that I had come to meet my "mentee."

Immediately, a young boy, who had been eyeing me the entire time from across the room, came and tugged on my trousers. The boy, eight years old, short, with glasses and a warm voice, was Charlie. He had been waiting all day to meet me. And he wasted no time asking questions, wanting to know every detail about my life. He was smarter and more conversational than I remember being at his age.

I had been nervous waiting to meet him. While I had been trained how to talk with children about domestic violence and identify the signs of new violence in the home, one can't be trained to develop a meaningful relationship with a child.

I hoped we would get along. But any initial doubts were gone after, having only just met me, Charlie gave me the sort of hug a child would give a father.

After meeting Charlie, I met his mother: a strong woman. She moved

Adopt an animal · Make a donation to my old school · Read for the blind

to Indiana to escape an abusive relationship, taking her four young children with her. The mother and I agreed Charlie and I were a good match, and from that point on, I was his mentor.

To Charlie, I am just a friend, someone he can trust and especially someone he can have fun with. After the first week picking up Charlie from school, hanging out with him, getting to know him, playing basketball or football with him, I was no longer scared about my new responsibility. Charlie did not expect me to drastically change his life. He did not see himself as a statistic or a figure in a column, as the Rise and especially the government does. He just wants to be a kid, and he makes sure whenever we get together, we have lots of fun.

This was important because Charlie did not always get to have the fun all kids should enjoy. His mom has to raise four kids on her own while taking classes on the side to get a college degree. She is a great mother and loves her children, but she does not have the time to give each of them the individual attention they need. So to Charlie, our meetings were special because he got particular attention and had a trusted friend to look after him.

It took very little time for him to start trusting me.

After picking him up from daycare one afternoon, I asked what he had learned in school that day. He responded that his class learned about the ozone. In a very adult tone, Charlie explained to me the dangers of a depleted ozone and its effects on the earth. He told me he was frightened that humans might die because the ozone is destroyed.

"I don't want to die from the ozone because I haven't even kissed a girl yet," he said.

It was such a simple conversation, but I will always remember it because it seemed like such a personal thought. I was touched that Charlie shared his observation with me. It showed me that he trusted and cared enough to tell me about something on his mind.

I hope I might have some impact on Charlie's life, but I have no illusions that when he goes on to do great things he will remember me. Instead, he has taught me a lot about my own life, and for that I am in Charlie's debt. For now I know that before I die, I want to have children of my own someday.

G I V E

CAUSES
When was the last time you voted?

COMMUNITY
Who has made the biggest positive impact on your life so far?

CAUSES
What's your definition of a "good cause"?

What's the best gift you ever received? The best one you ever gave?

Whom do you admire for his or her ideals?

Name one thing you would change about the education system.

Is there anyone you owe an apology to?

COMMUNITY
Name one person you know who might need your help right now.

CAUSES
Name something you think is worth fighting for.

COMMUNITY
Who embarrasses you with their generosity? How can you return the favor?

What would you want your children to believe in?

What's on Your List?

To "learn"

COMMUNITY — How well do you know your neighbors?

CAUSES — What recent story in the news has most shocked you?

COMMUNITY — Name a local organization whose aims you support.

Is there someone in your life who is difficult to forgive?

CAUSES — Global warming? Globalization? What do you feel is the most pressing problem we face today?

COMMUNITY — Name something or someone you know you take for granted.

CAUSES — What cause would you volunteer your time for?

Is the world a better place than it was 10 years ago?

What would you not sacrifice in order to make a difference?

Can violence ever be justified?

What project are you most proud to have been involved in?

CAUSES

No.50

PERFECT A MAGIC TRICK

LEARN

The need to know more ● Asking questions ● Taking notes ● Finding a mentor ● Exploring different points of view ● Swapping opinions with a friend ● Keeping informed ● Solving mysteries ● Teaching yourself ● Brushing up a skill ● Proving somebody wrong ● Picking up a new hobby ● Starting from scratch ● Cracking codes ● Connecting the dots...

51 Sing opera

Sandy, 55, Nantucket, MA

Today she called me adorable, then hit me. I am not in an abusive relationship — at least I hope not. I have merely taken up serious singing, at an age when, if I'd been serious to start with, I'd be calling it quits, and my teacher, several decades my senior, is a perfectionist who in her passion for music sometimes gets carried away. It's true that I was hunching my shoulders — a less than optimal way, instinct notwithstanding, to reach the high notes. Her swat was utterly justified.

My new obsession began innocently enough, with involvement in a community choir. Small semi-solos — quartets, trios, duets — have slowly led to this, my greatest challenge to date, singing the part of Gilda, Rigoletto's innocent young daughter who sacrifices herself in the name of love. "Caro nome" — "dear name" — is the aria I've been entrusted with, and it's a bitch, sprinkled with high Bs, Cs, and in its penultimate flourish a trill that dances even higher, in a range I would have thought audible only to dogs. It is one scary undertaking.

Every time I head over to Paulette's studio ("Breeze een!" her Swiss-accented admonitions haunt me. "Don't chute!"), I have to wonder how absurd my newfound ambition must seem, right up there with Zelda Fitzgerald taking up ballet in her thirties. How many good — or even passable — amateur years can I have left? And yet when I leave each lesson, I'm walking on air — "sull'aria," as the phrase goes in another selection we're preparing, a duet from *Figaro*.

> "I have to wonder how absurd my newfound ambition must seem."

Musical phrases pursue me throughout the day. It's all I can do not to burst into song while poring over mesclun in the supermarket. And alone in the car? Forget it — I'm Callas and Sutherland rolled into one, a blasting bundle of virtuosity.

My mother, a former concert violinist and dedicated non-athlete, took up tennis in her late sixties, so there's some precedent for this type of late-life mania. She got healthy and strong. I'm getting slowly pried out of shyness. If you want to sing, you can't lurk and hope to be overlooked. You have to put yourself out there, front and center. The only way I've found to do this is to imagine myself in service to the music. Ego comes into play, of course, but less as goad than stumbling block: stop to consider how you sound and you're sunk.

Performances invariably flash by in a sickening swoop, not unlike a ski slalom. Did you catch that breath? Uh-oh, too bad, forge ahead and don't take even a microsecond to berate yourself, it's too late. You emerge at the end so high on adrenaline, it takes ages to return to earth and remember where you are. At some point, with any luck, you managed to zombie-walk offstage.

You'd think the post-concert compliments would be the big payoff, but really the most rewarding part is when you're summoning the courage to get up and do this thing which your rational mind tells you you simply can't.

"Don't sink — just DO!" Paulette's voice infuses my every waking moment. I wish I'd met her decades ago. I'm glad to have her poking and prodding and praising me now, even if she does sometimes tend to get carried away. I'm starting to, too.

Learn to fly a plane
Mary, 46, Columbus, OH

I'd like to be able to say that I learned to fly an airplane at age 20 because of some lifelong dream. But that wasn't the case for me. The real drive that I had to get my pilot's license was a simple case of sibling rivalry. I wanted to teach my older brother a lesson he wouldn't soon forget.

It all began when I had an opportunity to fly in the copilot's seat of my dad's friend's private plane on a flight from the Bahamas to Florida. It was awesome, buzzing through the clouds, at first avoiding them like you do an unknown object on the road, before getting up the courage to poke the plane through one to see what they looked like from the inside.

Mr. Underwood, the pilot, told my dad I was a natural. It had been a lot of fun, but I really didn't think very seriously about it until I told my older brother the story, suggesting, "I think I'd like to learn to fly

Learn to fix my own car · Join a debate club · Take saxophone lessons

someday." He quickly responded with a condescending "You couldn't learn to fly a plane, there's a lot more to it than you think." His response didn't surprise me. I was, after all, "a girl" and his baby sister to boot. But I think my intense reaction surprised me. While my lips said, "Yeah, you're probably right," my mind was racing with the image of him in the backseat of a plane with me at the controls and him begging for mercy just before he threw up all over himself. I made a pledge to myself right then that I would learn to fly a plane.

I don't think a week passed before I enrolled in a private pilot ground school class at Ohio State University. I was already taking classes there at night and needed some electives, so I figured it couldn't hurt anything. I was also reading everything I could find on becoming a pilot. My favorite book was *The Joy of Learning to Fly*, which explained the importance of the relationship between the student and the instructor. Immediately after passing the ground school class, I began my flight training.

I was only 20 years old but was already two years older than my instructor. A male chauvinist like my brother, he acted like he had drawn the short straw when teamed up with the only woman in the class (so much for *The Joy of Learning to Fly*). My instructor seemed sure that it would take me twice the 40-hour minimum in flight hours to get my rating. If my motivation had been faltering at this point, it was once again rejuvenated. And after four months, 45 hours' flying time, and several near death experiences, I was officially a private pilot.

Mr. Underwood, the pilot from whom I'd gotten my start, was coaching me long distance via cards and the phone. When I had gotten lost flying from Dayton back to Columbus on only my second cross-country solo, the single most frightening experience of my life, it was Mr. Underwood's card that finally got me back in the air. It read: "The only pilots that haven't gotten lost are pilots who haven't flown anywhere."

I realized my other goal as well a few months later. My brother had a friend, Pete, who was a pilot with his own private plane. We decided that the three of us would take my sister for a short flight one sunny afternoon. Privately, I told Pete and my sister what my plan was. As we got to altitude, Pete gave me the controls in a very ceremonious fashion.

I remember he yelled to my brother in the backseat, "Don't worry, Paul, she's as good a pilot now as she ever will be."

At that moment, knowing I would never again have the opportunity to have my brother as a passenger, I pitched the plane into a severe 90 degree turn, followed by another in the opposite direction, then another and another. I will never forget the look on my brother's face.

For me, the thrill of learning to fly was not in any way diminished by what had originally motivated me to do it. It has single-handedly given me more confidence with everything I have tried to do thereafter than anything I can imagine doing.

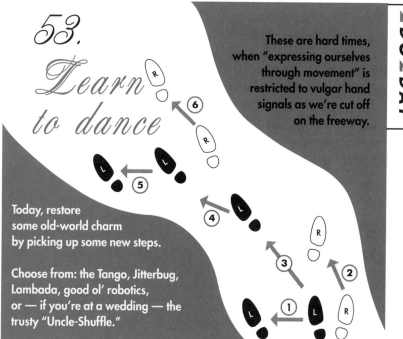

53.
Learn to dance

2DO2DAY

These are hard times, when "expressing ourselves through movement" is restricted to vulgar hand signals as we're cut off on the freeway.

Today, restore some old-world charm by picking up some new steps.

Choose from: the Tango, Jitterbug, Lambada, good ol' robotics, or — if you're at a wedding — the trusty "Uncle-Shuffle."

Study neuroscience · Take up astronomy · Put myself through college

54 Keep bees

Harry, 34, London

My second cousin John was a deep-sea diver and he kept bees. I was about ten when my mother told me about him. I remember being intrigued by the verb: keeping bees. Keeping them, as in not getting rid of them? Or keeping them against their will? Or what?

Obviously I knew honey came from bees, but how? That seemed to raise more questions than it answered. Was it straight from flowers or was it something made by the bees? And did it come from their mouths or their bottom or worse? Were bees happy to provide us with honey, and, if so, why? The very ordinariness of the stuff contrasted with the sheer mystery of its origin.

Four years ago I left my job and had to write a resume. I realized then I didn't have any hobbies, and I thought I had better acquire one. The family connection and the mystique about honey were suddenly recalled, and I identified beekeeping as my hobby-to-be. For a year I went to classes, read books on the subject, listened in to web chatrooms as apiarists swapped notes on swarms, yields, and diseases, and bought a protective veiled hat which I wore to a costume party. My family were excitedly hoarding empty jam-jars ready for the honey harvest to come. I showed off about my hobby and described myself as "pre-bee."

The next summer I built my hive, and for £50, bought a box of bees from a man who lived 20 miles away. I drove home with my protective veil on, a buzzing box in the trunk, inching over every pothole and bump in the road.

Three seasons later, I am still struggling to master beekeeping, but I can't imagine life without bees. The feeling of peacefulness as I spend an hour with my bees on a summer morning is unbeatable. Bees finished evolving 40 million years ago, while we humans were still sludgy toads: they are massively more perfected animals than we are, and they seem to know it. Seeing into their world is a privilege that even a dozen stings can't diminish. And, like a parent admiring nursery-school macaroni art, I am pathetically proud of my bees' handiwork. Nothing matches the taste of honey from my own bees.

Experience weightlessness - Speak Japanese - Read a book a week

55 Learn Italian
Emanuel, 36, Cleveland

When I was in third grade, I fell in love with French. I can remember Mr. Brooks's lesson as if it were yesterday. Counting to ten. The days of the week. And who could forget *fermer votre bouche* (shut your mouth)? But after two years of French in elementary school, I was still left with only a few phrases memorized. My mother could impress her friends when I'd regurgitate a few complete sentences in the language of love. But that's as far as it went.

Still, I wanted to become fluent in a second language. Being an African American, I knew that I couldn't base the choice on my cultural heritage. My ancestry was too far removed from Africa; and Ebonics was not an option.

My next exposure to foreign languages didn't come until I joined the Air Force in the nineties. After six months of active duty, I received the call to go to Desert Storm. While in Saudi Arabia and later Egypt, I managed to pick up a few phrases in Arabic from a few shop owners and cab drivers. But after six months in the area, all I remember is how to say "thank you."

Everything changed when I was assigned to a base in northern Italy. Living only forty-five minutes from Venice, I knew I had to try harder, be more than an ugly American who expected the natives to adhere to my language. And I didn't want to be one of those people who go to a bar and order a "glass of cow" by accident. I studied Berlitz tapes day and night. I asked locals for lessons. Finally, I took a college course that gave me the passion to learn more. But nothing was more helpful than living in the country for a year and learning from local folks and listening to radio and TV. By the time I left, I could keep up a pretty good conversation in Italian. I could even throw in a few slang words. I was hooked.

I still enjoy speaking the language, rolling my Rs while ordering the perfect dessert wine at a local Italian restaurant or picking up on a few sentences while watching the news in Italian on cable TV. But now, ten years later, my skills have gotten quite rusty.

The local community college offers classes in Italian. But with a

Play the harmonica · Become an expert on wine · Learn to windsurf

career and a family, it's difficult to fit one in my schedule. Plus, I used most of my G.I. Bill benefits on earning a degree in a more practical subject: Business. But before I die, I'm going to get back in those classes and become fluent. It's a promise I've made to myself that I plan to keep.

56- Graduate from college

Zina, 54, Bronx, NY

I grew up in the Bronx with a father who was a drinking bartender and a mother who had seven children and worked full-time at Woolworth's, so a college education was not a topic of discussion.

I married at 20 years of age and my husband frowned on my furthering my education. He didn't think I needed it, and we really could not afford it. But after being married for six years I enrolled in a city program for free college courses — just before I found out I was pregnant. My plans were canceled. I had to continue working. I also had a heart problem so it would have all been too much.

When my son was about 10 years old, I decided to try again. It lasted for 15 credits. At that point, my marriage was on the rocks and I had financial difficulties, so I had to put my aspirations to be a college graduate on hold once again.

Over the next ten years I started and stopped due to various setbacks with my health, but I finally did earn my degree two years after my son graduated from college. My goal had been to beat him to it — I was close enough!

I believe attending college as an adult allows you to really appreciate the education you are receiving and cherish the interaction with professional teachers. Several years have passed and I still smile when I think of my accomplishment.

Cook a meal

you've never made before

Whether it's baking bread, rolling your own sushi, or simply preparing lobster thermidor for a party of 12, try learning something new in the kitchen today.

58   Find a faith

Moshe, 33, Alon Shevut, Israel

At age 18, on the first day of college, I was asked if I was Jewish. I replied, "No, but my parents are." I was a biological Jew. I wasn't resentful of my Jewish upbringing, I just didn't practice.

But something happened over the next five years, and at age 23 I found myself heading to Israel for the first time, on my way to study in a Yeshiva. It doesn't get any more Jewish than Yeshiva, the place where one throws oneself entirely into studying, living, and attempting to understand all that the Jewish tradition has had to say over the last 4,000 years.

Somehow or other, I had gone from being totally uninterested in religion in general, and my own in particular, to finding religion the single most important force in my life.

But why? The answer, albeit a partial one, lies in a simple institution known as the Shabbas Table. The Shabbas Table is exactly as its name implies. It's a table where one sits and eats with friends and family on Shabbas. And yet contained within this simple institution is a simple truth that sent my life in a new direction. At least, that's how I experienced it one Friday night more than a decade ago. It was a night that seemed so normal, and yet its normality was what made it so special.

For all of my life, Friday had revolved around the question, "What are we going to do tonight?" But this Shabbas night I found myself with five normal, interesting, witty, and intelligent people sitting around a table just enjoying themselves. No one had anywhere to go. There was no pressure to leave, or to do something else. Indeed, this is what Shabbas helped me to see: "What are we going to do tonight?" was the wrong question. The real question is "*Who* am I going to spend my time with tonight?"

From that night on, that anxiety was removed from my consciousness. I knew exactly what I was going to do. I was going to go to synagogue and then have a Shabbas dinner. I didn't have to worry about parties or functions. I didn't have to wonder if somehow or other I was missing it — you know "it," that nebulous something that exists only in our minds. That was no longer part of my world the moment I took

Shabbas on. It was a complete change of focus for me. Shabbas was about *who* as opposed to *what*, people rather than events. It was that change in focus that drew me in and has kept me in ever since.

Play the drums
59 Tim, 30, London

Maybe it's something deeply primal — or perhaps linked to a fetish for large wooden objects covered in colored vinyl, I'm not sure — but all I know is that there is nothing on this planet remotely like smacking seven shades of shit out of a well-worn, well-tuned drum kit. Particularly, for some reason, when old people are present — which, along with the sheer pleasure of always being the loudest one in the room, somehow makes up for the aching limbs, bad back, and escalating deafness. It also makes up for the fact that while all other band members are happily engaged in the post-gig drinking/scoring ritual, the drummer is perpetually out in the back, packing the van. Having performed other musical roles in my time, I can also report that no other instrument so often prompts the comment, "Oh, I've always wanted to have a go at that" — or more specifically, "You know, I reckon I'd make a great drummer." OK, so what's stopping you?

Probably a number of things. The cost, the noise levels, the time it would take up, the feeling that you're far too old and that the notion of learning an instrument is somehow confined to those below the age of twelve. All of which, I need hardly tell you, is complete bollocks.

For a start, be realistic. There's no point in forking out on a drum kit before you've tried it. Everyone has a friend, or even a friend of a friend, with some drums, so get yourself invited round for tea and then slip the drum owner a fiver to bugger off down to the pub for an hour while you acquaint yourself with his/her precious instruments (I know this will work, because every drummer in the world is both broke and an alcoholic). If this introductory session bores you rigid, go no further. If not, get yourself a small set of drums.

You don't need to spend too long practicing — fifteen minutes per

Study Greek philosophy · Know my rights · Print photos in a darkroom

day is perfectly reasonable and unlikely to make you that unpopular with the neighbors — but make it regular. If you're frustrated that you're not progressing, now might be the time for a teacher; but equally, get the friend whose drums you first played to come round once every couple of weeks, watch you play, and make some suggestions in return for a few beers (with the added bonus that you'll be making the drummer feel important — or useful even).

The final, essential hurdle on your road to Percussion Mecca is joining a band. This may induce spasms of fear, but believe me — nothing will sharpen your drumming skills like playing with other musicians. The classified ads are full of often appalling outfits searching for a drummer; go and audition, ignoring the nerves, the logistical difficulties, and the relentless sarcasm. Having been both the auditionee and auditioner numerous times over the years, I can tell you that it's highly unlikely you will be the worst drummer they've seen that day.

Alternatively, form your *own* group; possibly grab a few work colleagues who say stuff like "I used to play guitar," go down to a rehearsal room, and just play. Don't worry too much about the sound that comes out. Remember that even U2 started with a garage rehearsal during which no actual chords were played. The only one who could vaguely play their instrument? Larry Mullen, the drummer. Coincidence? I think not.

And as for being too old, I've never heard such balls. Let me tell you: at the ripe old age of thirty, I have never needed drumming so much. The older one gets, the more stressful life becomes, and no instrument relieves stress more accurately than the drums. Besides, some of the world's most prominent drummers — Buddy Rich, Charlie Watts, Mick Fleetwood, even John Bonham — have always looked absolutely ancient, even when they were in their early twenties.

My last, and perhaps most valid, point on the subject is that in the history of light entertainment, has there ever been a character so energetic, so hilarious, so closely observed, so perfectly conceived, so carelessly bonkers, and so downright cool as Animal, the drummer from the Muppets? Never. With a little effort, you too could be like Animal from the Muppets. And what more could you want from life than that?

60 Learn to swim

Michael, 26, Carbondale, IL

When I was born, a congenital defect meant that I would never be able to walk unless the good doctors at the University of Iowa hospital fused my anklebones at right angles. The result is that to this day, a limp that is only slightly noticeable on sidewalks keeps me out of the water altogether.

But all of my life I've watched friends swim like silver-backed koi under the waters of lakes and swimming pools, and I would want, if I had a very limited time left on this earth, to join them.

There was one weekend, however, when I came closest to learning how to swim. It was several months after my mother died, and my father took the family on a short cruise in the Bahamas. It was the vacation my mother had always wanted — but missed — so it felt both appropriate and oddly obscene to be there without her. But it also seemed to me to be the perfect time to face my fear of water.

One afternoon while we were visiting a tiny uninhabited island, I slipped off behind two bent coconut trees and changed into swim trunks I had not planned on using. I made sure no one was watching — least of all a family member who would probably think I was either insane or suicidal — and walked further and further out on the sands.

When I got to the water, it was warmer than I'd imagined, and I waded in past my thighs, then up to my navel. Then I went further, until the water was lapping at my sternum. By now I was starting to panic as my feet slid on the wet sands underneath, but I took a deep breath, bent my knees, and lowered my face beneath the water.

The first thing I was aware of was my heart pounding like a kettle-drum, as if I were a child again, sinking my ears under the bathwater.

But this was different. When I opened my eyes, I saw white shafts of sunlight scattering over shells and sand and colored pebbles. In the distance I could see tiny fish of various metallic hues moving either in short fluttery gestures or long ballet-like strokes across their sea-stage. Already crouching, I sank even further and watched them, and the water closed in over the top of my head. I had only that one breath in my lungs, but my sense of panic had faded so my heartbeat slowed, and it went on like I was watching them for hours.

I tried to look past those titanium-like fins and the occasional spider-legged shrimp to what lay beyond. I knew that, further out, the sandy floor dropped and turned to rock, and the wilder regions of the ocean began. And I knew that if I could swim, if I could go out far enough, I might find whales drifting like ancient blimps, plus sharks and dolphins too. A whole world I had seen only in pictures.

My air was running out. I lifted my head and felt the water run from my body. I took my first painful breath under the sun. I wanted to go back, to at least try kicking and fanning my arms as I'd seen Olympic swimmers do on TV, but suddenly the notion seemed silly.

I turned and waded back onto the beach, returning to my family and the flocks of tourists. Shivering in a new faint chill, wondering if I'd ever return to try all of it again.

Pass on a skill

Hana, 23, Chicago

When my mother first proposed connecting Grandma to cyberspace, I tried to hide the horror flashing through my mind.

The last time I talked with my grandmother about the Internet, I hardly got a word in. How did it start? How did it work? Where did the information go? What about hackers? Is it safe? Who puts the World Wide Web together? Can you see the same pages from different computers? Do you think this is good for society? How is it helping people? Do you think computers are replacing jobs? Boy, in my day...

I did, however, admire my grandmother for her curiosity and interest in the modern world. Thus, on her most recent visit, I succumbed to her

Learn to fly-fish · Plant a garden · Look at the stars through a telescope

request to "learn" the Internet. I found myself in my parents' office, trying to show her the basics, and forgot that would include Windows, using a mouse ("Eek!" she said, "why would someone call it a mouse?"), watching her be patient because it was slow and amazed because it was so fast, and listening to the beeps, clicks, taps, and chimes.

"But how, Hana, how?" Grandma persists.

"I don't know, it just does. Look it up on the Internet. Find out how the Internet works on the Internet. Go to a search engine."

"Do you always go to a search engine?" she asks.

"Uh, when I am searching for stuff I do."

"Be patient, Hana, be patient." This is the line Grandma always tells me when she does not like my "tone."

I begin to feel guilty for not being a better teacher. I take several deep breaths, and vow to be more patient. The technology was truly amazing, and understandably complex to someone who grew up when Model T's were all the rage.

She is fumbling with the mouse, the way first-time users do, as if it is uncontrollable and foreign. She tries on three pairs of glasses before she finds the ones that allow her to best read the screen. She asks for help in adjusting the chair, in turning on the fan (there is one switch on the fan, one), and then looks at me, with eyes she must have seen on me years ago when she took me on my first trip to Disneyland, and says, "Okay, thanks, Hana, you can leave now."

I left her to explore the World Wide Web, and I felt strangely satisfied at the accomplishments, both hers and mine. I was actually happy to be the one to show Grandma the wonders of the World Wide Web. I realized one day my grandchildren will painstakingly show *me* the newest technology or the newest planet, for that matter, and I too will have four million questions.

Name one skill you could learn that would benefit your career.

What's the most recent thing someone has taught you?

If you could get an honest answer to any one question, what would you ask?

Name one evening class you would like to take with your partner.

Which period in history are you curious to know more about?

What one scientific discovery would you most like to see in your lifetime?

Name a foreign language you would like to speak fluently.

Name one thing you could teach someone else how to do.

Name a skill you can't imagine living without.

Name a musical instrument you would like to play.

What's on

LEARN

To "Express"

Your List?

Name one thing you wish you could learn instantly.

Who are your hero's heroes?

What subject has proved the most/least useful since leaving high school?

Name a skill a friend of yours has that you admire.

Name a skill you already have, but would like to improve.

Do you believe in "genius"?

If you could pass on one piece of advice to your 15-year-old self, what would it be?

What book would you recommend others read?

No.62
PAINT ON A LARGE CANVAS

EXPRESS

Speaking your mind • Trusting your gut • Dismissing doubts • Taking risks • Getting up on stage • Braving failure • Staring at a blank canvas • Being inspired • Finding a voice • Cracking a joke • Doodling in the margins • Writing the first lines • Going to the opening night • Setting yourself apart • Collaborating with others • Digging deep • Keeping your nerve...

Perform stand-up comedy
David, 42, San Rafael, CA

The first time I heard Lenny Bruce I was already in college and he was already dead. Lenny Bruce didn't exist in the America where I grew up. Everyone was too busy worshipping Bear Bryant and voting for George Wallace and worrying about how to keep the "colored people" out of their schools.

So at 20, when I first laid ears on Mr. Bruce spinning out his Lone-Ranger-and-Tonto-Perform-an-Unnatural-Act bit, a choir of angels and devils sang to me, and lo the Muse didst fill me with the sweetest white light and yeah I saw me a vision: David Henry Sterry, on stage, microphone in hand, cracking up the masses with my masterful stand-up.

Then I pictured the highly acclaimed comedy albums; the small but influential role of the young, angry but very funny Vietnam vet opposite Marlon Brando; the Best Supporting Actor Oscar acceptance speech that's an instant classic: the world roars at my scything wit, I make the glitterati rethink their world views on hunger, poverty, and abuse, and I propose a viable solution, while still finding time to thank all the little people, all in under four minutes. When I leave the stage waving the Oscar over my head, they roar, oh how they roar.

Now all I had to do was write an act. You know, some jokes. How hard could it be? Took me 3½ years to write five minutes of material. But I did it. Timed it and everything. I didn't work out an encore. Figured I'd just go out and ad lib when they called me back. I didn't really know what ad lib was, but I figured by the time I got done with my killer five minutes, I would.

So on a Monday night, in the post-Mork mid-eighties San Francisco stand-up comedy boom, I went down to the Holy City Zoo at 6 p.m. And there, I signed up on the List. Only I was so sure I was going to blow and bite that I made up a name. Franklin P. Funk. Don't ask. When they posted the list at 7:30ish, I had the 1:20 a.m. slot. But the guy told me not to be surprised if I got bumped.

By 10 o'clock the tiny, sweaty joint was packed way beyond the rafters as the headliners rocked and rolled the house. They made it look so easy, just talking to some drunk, or telling some stupid story, or making some crazy face. I can do this, I thought, my stuff is way funnier than most of the lame stuff everybody's yucking it up over.

By 1 o'clock things weren't looking so pretty. There were twelve drunks, nineteen angry, bitter, insecure, maniacally competitive wannabe comics, and one guy who kept muttering a little loud about aliens and probes and how he wasn't going to take it anymore. By 1:15 I was convinced that this was a very bad idea, that my material was horrible, that I was going to fail, be heckled and jeered, then blown off the stage, fleeing in tail-between-legs disgrace.

Then I saw it: the ghost of Lenny Bruce. Changing the world one joke at a time. In my head I heard his Tonto say, "I want Tanta the Indian! To perform an unnatural act!" And I cracked up. Just then the emcee said: "I don't know who this next guy is, but uh... weird name... Franklin P. Funk."

For a second I forgot that was my stage name. Then I remembered: "Damn! That's me!" I raced up on stage and launched right into my bit. No: "Hello, how are ya?" No: "Hi, my name is suchandsuch." Nothing. Just blasted into a five-minute rant about some never-identified product that did all kinds of undoable things for you: clean your uterus, sanitize your testicles so they feel feminine fresh. It was to be the five longest minutes of my life. I had no way of knowing that as I launched into it. I thought my scathing indictment on the evils of capitalism subconsciously enslaving consumers by making them want things they don't even need through vilifying the human body in hideous insidious erotophobic post-Puritan ways was going to KILL.

At first, a few people laughed. Especially this one drunk guy. And when he laughed a few other drunk guys laughed. People are funny that way. But after about a minute or so everybody stopped laughing. Even the laughing drunk guy. At two minutes in, I became acutely aware of every sound. It was like I was hearing the soundtrack for the movie of this scene, only the ambient sounds were turned up way too high: clearing throats and rest-

Have a photo exhibition · Audition for a play · Compose a film score

less shifting buttocks, clinking drinks, muttered chuckles of comics mocking me to each other under their breath, alien probe rumblings, the slamming of the door as a drunk staggers out in disgust, all driven by the rhythm of my relentless pounding telltale heart.

Here is a wonderful example of the Relativity Theory: the next minute lasted more than 2½ years.

Three minutes in I'm sweat-drenched yet clammy-cold. There's a technical term for this in Stand-Up nomenclature: "Flop Sweat."

Four minutes in I lost my place. Sadly, I realized it didn't actually matter; they had no idea what I was talking about anyway. I just picked up somewhere else in the bit, and I resumed plummeting like the pilot of a plane with its engines on fire, nowhere to go but down to a fiery crash and burn. Finally, mercifully, the emcee came and stood by the exit to the stage. That's your sign: Time's up, Bub.

So I stopped. And we all stared at each other. Me, the drunks, the bitter insecure comics, even the alien probe guy. And in that silence I said: "Wow, that kinda sucked, huh?"

I just said it. Cuz that's what I was thinking. Cuz it was so utterly the truth.

Everyone laughed. Drunkards, angry wannabe comics, alien probe man, even the cynical seen-way-too-much-of-this emcee. And as the glorious wave of laughter showered me with all that endorphin-rich, adrenalizing love, there it was again: the ghost of Lenny Bruce, smiling at me.

Then I said: "Thank you very much, you've been a great crowd!" Like I just killed when actually I just really sucked. And I got that oh so beautiful laugh-on-a-laugh, the topper laugh, and my goodness did it feel good as I flowed through the crowd strangely flushed with that tiny victory in the face of all that stinking bombing suckage.

I did stand-up every night for the next year. Three months after my most painful comedy cherry popping, I was offered my first paying gig. Six months later, I was making an extremely meager living as a stand-up. My friend Len, who was a great comic and is now clinically insane, claims that any idiot can make his living at stand-up. All he has to do is perform every night for one year. I am living proof that this is true.

Give a lecture · Make a movie · Paint an altarpiece · Win a debate

64   Get a tattoo

Kevin, 32, San Francisco

I'm not much of a man of deeds and actions, I guess I'm more a man of statements (read: "lazy know-it-all"). But look on my right hip — and a few other places, now that some years have passed and more trips to the parlor have been made — and you'll see something to set me apart, just a little bit.

When I first started thinking about getting a tattoo at the age of fifteen, there were only two things holding me back from taking my fake ID and heading to the wonderful and lively downtown area of Springfield, Massachusetts, for a session with the resident biker thug/tattoo artist: 1. I didn't have a clue what I wanted, and 2. it seemed wrong to just "get a tattoo." I had it in my head that it should mark an occasion in my life, something life changing, perhaps, or at the very least a moment to be remembered. That way, when my memory began giving out I could look down at my body and say, "Oh yeah, I got that one when I left home," or, "Hey, that was the night I won the Oscar for Best Set Design," or even, "Ah yes, my first night in prison. What memories!"

It took a while for the right moment to present itself, but I finally decided that a dual occasion was appropriate. When I was 22, I graduated college and moved to San Francisco. I figured it was my duty to mark both the end of eighteen years of hellish, useless education and the beginning of living in one of the best cities on the planet.

> "I had it in my head that it should mark an occasion in my life."

In search of an appropriate design, I turned to Hunter S. Thompson, my guru and spiritual leader in those days. Sure enough, a design on page one of his book *The Great Shark Hunt* jumped out at me — a two-thumbed hand holding a peyote button. A suitably twisted design from the great journalist.

When I got to San Francisco, I began to ask a few of my more marked-up friends and found a properly seedy joint in the lower Haight district. The first time I thought of getting the tattoo I made the mistake

Write a letter to the editor · Draw a comic strip · Spend the day naked

of telling my dad, whose anti-ink sentiments I had severely underestimated. He tried to deter me, saying it would be by far the most painful experience of my life. He hadn't swayed me, but his words had stuck in my mind, so I had a couple of cocktails before going in, to help ease the pain. Plus, this was a special morning. I wasn't about to go to Starbucks and get a latte and a muffin.

My first thought as I walked into the place was that the tattoo artist looked like he'd had a rough night — if he'd had a night at all. It certainly didn't look like he'd had a morning. It may not seem physically possible for a guy with a shaved head and a tank top to look disheveled, but he'd pulled it off. I hesitated, but only for a brief moment. This guy's a professional, right? So I gave him the design and he went to work on my right hip.

The choice of location was easy. This tattoo was personal, so I didn't want to share it with just anyone. I'd show it to the people I wanted to and keep it secret from everyone else. So I picked a spot just below the belt line, right under the big scar I got playing street hockey in high school.

People may tell you differently, but give me a tattoo over a trip to the dentist anytime. It took about an hour and the pain from the needle wasn't that bad. I was pleased that the guy had finished it before passing out or dying. He had done a brilliant job. It was everything I had imagined it to be.

I hadn't gotten to choose anything else about my body (being in shape, having long hair, and other fleeting crap doesn't count) but I had chosen this. I didn't know how I'd feel about the tattoo once I was staring at it every day. But nearly ten years later, it feels more right than I ever thought it would.

65 DRAW A SELF-PORTRAIT

It doesn't matter if you think you're good or bad at drawing. Today, hark back to your days of free-form finger painting and sketch yourself without even a glance at the paper.

66 Stage a play

Kate, 29, London

When we planned it, it sounded as though it would be fun, easy, unstressful — I mean, how could something so inherently light-hearted, in which the principal comedy comes from men dressed in drag and villains being followed by a green spotlight and a smoke effect, possibly be stressful? Surely this would be simple.

A word at this stage about exactly the type of thing we had decided to write. I like to call it a "show" now — this gives it a glamorous Broadway musical air and implies a level of professionalism that is healthy for my sense of well-being. What we had in fact decided to write was a "pantomime," basically a peculiar fairy tale with bad jokes and lots of songs. The audience is encouraged to participate rowdily in cheering the heroes and booing the bad guy. In other words, it's all actually quite silly.

Get an agent · Be a street performer · Design a T-shirt · Direct a musical

What followed were some of the scariest months of my life. First, I had to write a full-length script for our chosen show, *Cinderella*. This was something that I had never done before, and it took me several false starts before I finally managed to get going. I was such an inexperienced scriptwriter that I initially found it very hard to separate the good ideas from the bad — I became attached to particular bits of dialogue and secondary plot ideas, and did not have the common sense to cut them.

As we went through the rehearsal process, a lot of this chaff was lost (and unfortunately for the final production some of it wasn't), but it would have caused considerably less heartache to the actors whose lines were being cut if I had just noticed that the lines were shockingly bad a month or so earlier.

Secondly, we had to find a cast. This is not that easy to do when a) you're not paying anyone, b) you are a completely untested writer, and c) everyone has a full-time job. Happily, many of my friends were willing to make fools of themselves in the name of charity (and helping me out). Even more happily for me, quite a lot of them are decent actors, so I knew that at least the acting wouldn't be horribly embarrassing, even if the script turned out to be exactly that.

Third, we had to find a venue, rehearsal rooms, producers, lighting people, sound people, set designer, costume designer, program designer... the list just went on. Plus, we had to find money to pay for all of this.

Finally, of course, we had to direct and stage the show. And then keep the cast sober during the performances, which I have to say proved a bridge too far for me.

"Before I went on I was shaking like a leaf."

It was a huge effort, from a huge number of people, that finally got my friend Susannah's and my first ever joint show onto the stage. We were both appearing in it as well, and before I went on I was shaking like a leaf, from the abject fear of failure (and an almighty adrenaline surge). But the feeling I got at the first laugh from the audience (which happened exactly on cue after the first joke) was incomparable. It's one thing to decide to write a show. It's another thing to actually do it. And when an audience clearly enjoys the show — laughing in all the right places, clapping along to all the songs, and cheering wildly at the end — it truly feels like nothing else I have ever experienced. On top of all that, we raised nearly $10,000 for charity, which can't be bad.

"It took some guts and extreme foolishness to put on that first pantomime."

As for the differences that all this has made to my life… it's really a case of where to start. By the time of our second production, I had decided that being a lawyer was no longer for me. I resigned my well-paid job and spent six months writing a book — it's nowhere near being picked up for publication, but I'm nonetheless proud of myself for producing it, and haven't given up hope that I can get it to a publishable stage. The musicals are going from strength to strength, and I have been asked to write a show for someone else, someone who has seen my work and enjoyed it. My first-ever commission.

Whether I keep writing and make this a career or decide that ultimately there's something to be said for going back to the boring yet predictable life of a lawyer, I know that there are people out there who have seen my shows, laughed at my jokes (out loud, sometimes), and paid money for the privilege. Some have even come back for more.

It took some guts and extreme foolishness to put on that first pantomime, but it has changed my life in ways I could never have predicted, and I wouldn't change that for the world.

67 Sing in a band
Jennifer, 29, Thousand Oaks, CA

I had always dreamed of being Stevie Nicks when I was a teenager. It wasn't necessarily just being her, more about performing. I watched concert footage of Stevie over and over again. I read interviews. I watched clips from rehearsals. And what I realized was that Stevie had complete control over her audience. She was the epitome of what I thought I should be.

But I had one problem: With the exception of piano lessons I took when I was in elementary school, I didn't know if I had any musical ability whatsoever. In seventh grade, when I took chorus, I couldn't open my mouth out of fear I would sound stupid. I lip-synched while everyone else sang. In cars with friends, I couldn't sing along to what we were listening to. The most I could do was sing to my dog about what she was going to have for dinner — I wouldn't let anyone hear my real voice.

"Just go out there," my friends told me. "Go to an audition. You won't know until you try."

"Oh, I don't know," I'd say, or, "There's no opportunities out there!" It was easier to keep the fantasy at bay than actually do something with it, so I didn't even try.

All the same, I kept at my fantasy. I got married and settled into suburban life, but still had a fascination with bands and female singers. I'd be drying the dishes, looking out into my backyard, and would imagine myself dancing on stage, a tambourine in my hand.

Then the opportunity came.

My husband worked in a law office with an attorney who was in a band. One summer, we watched his band perform on the Fourth of July. It was a sweltering day and the band played outdoors, despite the heat. The lead singer — a woman — belted out Led Zeppelin songs with no effort. Everyone in the audience sat in rapt attention watching them perform. It was a small venue, just a party, but there were enough people that it felt like a little concert.

"I could do that," I told my husband, half believing it. And for almost a year after, I did — in my head. I imagined myself joining the band, but didn't actually take any steps to pursue it. I decided I would do better as a backup singer, so I began learning the backup

Paint a mural · Keep a sketchbook · Cross-dress

parts to all of my favorite songs. I sang in the car and I even tried the shower. When cars would pass me on the street, instead of stopping the singing so that they wouldn't see me behaving like an idiot, I kept on going. Something inside me was breaking down.

One day, my husband mentioned to his colleague that I was interested in singing backup. He was intrigued. "Tell her to come to our next practice and we'll see what happens," he said.

When my husband called and told me, my heart dropped into my stomach and I started sweating. "Oh, I don't know," I said. "I have a sore throat." Which was true.

"You can go to the next one, then," my husband said. "They have practices every Monday night. It's really casual. They just want to have fun."

"I'll see," I told him.

That whole week, I couldn't think of anything else. I kept imagining myself up there on stage. What if I was horrible? What if I got there and couldn't open my mouth? What if I did open my mouth and horrible sounds came out? What if everyone laughed at me? As if I were a real singer! I was a fake, a wannabe, someone who had fallen in love with the image, not someone who was actually talented.

The next Monday came and I was fine. No sore throat. I had no excuse. All day at work, I couldn't focus. I kept imagining myself at the practice: failing. On the way, I got stuck in traffic. I banged my head on the steering wheel. "Maybe it's a sign," I kept thinking. "Maybe I shouldn't do it."

"What if I was horrible? What if I got there and couldn't open my mouth?"

When I eventually pulled up to the garage we were practicing in, everyone was sitting around drinking beer and eating pizza. I recognized the man who was now the lead singer and was introduced to everyone else in the band. When they began their practice, they just launched into "Honky-Tonk Blues."

"Oh no," I thought to myself. "This is it."

Then I did it. I joined in the chorus, opening my mouth wide, letting it all come out. To my surprise, no one laughed. In fact, both the bass guitarist and the lead singer nodded in approval. I tried to act like I knew what I was doing, grabbing the microphone by the base and singing directly into it. The guitarists played around me; the drums pounded and clashed. "I'm here," I thought. And it didn't seem bad, or unfamiliar. It was just something I was doing, like brushing my teeth or driving my car. The song ended. "Good," the lead singer said. "Let's try another one."

When the practice wrapped up at nine o'clock, the lead singer turned to me. "So, you'll be back next week?" he asked.

"You're saying I didn't suck?" I said casually.

"No, not at all."

"I'll get better, I promise."

"That's why we have practices," he said. "We just love to do it and we have fun. That's what matters."

The little me in my head, the one that always told myself I was horrible, started jumping up and down and cheering. On the outside, though, I remained composed. "Cool, then," I said, trying to sound nonchalant. "I'll see you next week."

"Work on singing louder," he called after me as I walked to my car.

"I will!" I yelled back.

I got in my car, turned on the ignition, turned the radio up loud, and sang all the way home. My back was covered in sweat. I felt like a giant weight had been lifted from my shoulders. A band. I was a backup singer in a real, live band.

A few months later, on the Fourth of July, I sang with the band in front of a crowd for the very first time. Maybe someone else was watching me, thinking, If that girl can do it, so could I.

No.68 Give a speech

" Whether it's a bit of soapbox sermonizing or a toast at the dinner table, stand up and have your say today. "

69 Open an underground arts club

Eric, 34, Columbus, OH

With one hand up the devil's ass and the smell of peroxide from the hair salon above assaulting my nostrils, I felt there must be a better venue for our particular brand of self-expression.

After a year of nonstop performance, bemusing audiences with philosophical Punch & Judy puppet shows and sociopolitical plays in the back rooms of bars and the basements of hair salons, my partner and I were getting tired of being *literally* underground.

And so we hatched a scheme to open a venue, a giant test tube for the mutant cultures of alternative and experimental expression that seemed to be evolving everywhere in the Gay Old '90s. Everyone was supposed to be busy making money, but everyone we knew was busy making art that they had nowhere to show or perform. Including ourselves.

After two years and a string of productions that cracked (if not conquered) the consciousness of the mainstream, giving us an air of quasi legitimacy in the process, we found the perfect theater. Except that it wasn't a theater at all. It was an old commercial garage, replete with the

Have a photo exhibition - Audition for a play - Compose an opera

residue of indoor oil slicks, restrooms that even the boldest Porta Pottie spelunkers would shun, and a "Valvoline Room" sign hanging on the office door.

It was love at first sight.

So what if we had no financial backing and little business plan besides "do what you love, help others do the same, and the rest will take care of itself"?

So what if this wasn't New York or Chicago, but was instead Columbus, Ohio — the sixteenth largest city in the country, a city dominated by rabid sports fanaticism that subsumed everything else in its wake?

So what? The artists we knew needed a place to call home, and the city needed a place to hear new voices, whether it knew it or not.

So what. Do or die. Grow or decay. Jump off the precipice and hope that something (or someone) is there to catch you — even if sometimes it's nothing more than your own ego, bruised and swollen to pillow-like proportions by the barrage of outrageous fortune and misfortune.

Four months and what seemed like four hundred gallons of paint later, with rent and renovations eating up my credit card, we opened the facility with a Halloween party in the middle of May. The next two years were a whirlwind of writing, performing, booking, fund raising, and creative financing. (We often jokingly refer to the theater as "the house that rave built," because we probably wouldn't have made it through that first phase without staying up all night to babysit the building through a plenitude of "private parties.")

"So what if this wasn't New York or Chicago?"

In short, it was one of the most ebulliently brutal times of my life. We hosted avant-garde jazz from Japan, salacious circuses from New York City, throat singers from Tuva, and some performance art that was a little weird even by *our* standards. All while creating our own shows and maintaining the commitment to provide an affordable outlet for local theater, performance, and visual art.

And, slowly, it caught on. It was as if all the malcontents and marginalized were just waiting for their very own clubhouse amid the meat markets and hipster hangouts and sports bars. A place that could be cool because it didn't give a shit about being cool. A place they could call home because here they *were* the mainstream.

And so they came, as they still do to this day, years after most people in the community thought we'd probably be forced to call it a day. And although we never really changed what we do, these days even more traditional audiences venture into our "funky downtown space," as the daily paper constantly referred to it during the first couple years. I guess everyone needs a little funk in their lives.

I'm not sure I'll ever have kids, but I know I have one big conceptual child that serves as a living playground to all the neighborhood playmates. Our organization has helped jump-start hundreds of micro-careers in the arts — not necessarily the kind of work that leads to a lot of money, but the more important work that provides a sense of purpose and fulfillment. We've helped stir up the cultural and political dialogue in our corner of the country. And, most important, we've built a home for ideas and for those who hatch them, for the avant-garde who may one day become the mainstream, and for the mainstream who need a little dose of adventure to shake up their souls.

70 — MAKE YOUR OWN CLOTHES

Don't like what the shopping mall has to offer? Break the mold with some clothes of your own.

You don't need a sewing machine — start with a marker. Customize a T-shirt, cut up jeans, dye your own socks... The possibilities are endless.

2DO2DAY

Get published

Carol, 53, Washington, DC

I am a writer." I've never written that before, but I've said it. I tried it out last year on Ralph, the wallpaper man. He was working in my bathroom and I was working at my computer. He stopped papering for a minute to get a drink of water and said to me, "Oh, are you a writer?"

A thousand thoughts flew through my mind: "He's only the wall-paper man." "He'll never know." "He doesn't know anyone I know." "It won't hurt anyone for me to say that I am what I wish I was." So I said, "Yes." Then I held my breath.

Then he said, "Oh, what do you write?"

I felt like you feel when you say something in a foreign language — and then they say something back — and then you have to hurry off to get another drink. But I was out on a limb, so I said, "Uh, I write personal essays." Then I pretended to be very busy.

A few days later I went to look for a new car. As we were strolling around, the car salesman casually asked, "What do you do?" Did I dare? I got away with it the first time.

This time it was easier. I said, "I'm a writer" — with a big smile. Then he said, "Oh, are you published?" This seemed to me to be a rude and uncalled-for question, since I think it must be implicit that if you say you're a writer, you must be published. Who would have the nerve to say they're a writer if they aren't even published?

While I'm not above stretching the truth to take on the persona of a self-confident author, I didn't have the nerve to say that I was published, since I knew what the next question would be. I also didn't want to find myself driving home a new car just to keep from answering. So I said, "Well, my husband says that I'm self-published."

"Oh," he said, "what does that mean?"

"I think it means that I'm not published." I told him I had an important appointment and left — without a car.

It was now clear to me that "I'm a writer" was not going to fly alone. Not even in a car dealership. In order to say two sentences about what I do, I was going to have to answer the question, "*Where* are you published?"

Do an impression - Visit the Prado gallery in Madrid - Body-paint

Slowly I came to life and began to send some of my things around to papers and magazines, and I attempted to find an agent.

I started feeling like a real writer when I realized what real writers do. Real writers are *re*writers. (Mark Twain said that the difference between the right word and the wrong word was the difference between "lightning" and "lightning bug.") I felt like a writer when I began to think of everything else to do besides rewrite, including go out of town. I cleaned out my closets, arranged all the photographs in an album, walked the legs off my dog, and redecorated the house. I detoured around the room where the dreaded essay sat.

I see why writers drink and smoke — it's something else to do. I see why writers are always having a dialogue with themselves. Between smoking, drinking, and talking to yourself, you can stay pretty busy.

But eventually your fingers wind up on that keyboard again and you rewrite and then rewrite some more. And then someone finally says "yes." Lily Tomlin once said, "I always wanted to *be* somebody, but now I see I should have been more specific." I've been specific for a long time. I've always wanted to be a writer — a published writer. And now, if you're reading this, I guess that I *am* one.

 ## Record an album
Michael, 32, London

My first band — at the age of nine — had an inauspicious debut. Grand dreams of selling tickets to the entire neighborhood quickly fell by the wayside when we — the mighty "Spiders of the Night" — had to beg a handful of babysitters, their kids, a few stray dogs, and some very patient parents to let us entertain them. How the world was rocked! Or not, rather.

Still, I wasn't put off. Scribbling songs into my teens, in the margins of my school notebooks and on napkins over dinner, I had hopes of one day producing something of worth that could capture people's ears, just as my musical heroes had captured mine. As the years went by, though, instead of writing songs, I got better and better at coming up with reasons why I shouldn't.

Rent a studio space · *Design a hat* · *Own a Robert Crumb original*

Years later, though, I spent an afternoon with my grandfather that changed my mind. My grandfather was dying, and in what turned out to be the last time we saw each other, he noted many of his regrets. Specifically, he spoke of things he'd started and allowed to gather dust. It was easy to imagine that one day I'd be in his position, head full of things I wish I had done.

So when I made my list of things to do before *I* was gathering dust, a few items stood out. One of these was "record an album." Just writing it down made my heart beat faster. That old fantasy, I thought...still, now that I was armed with a fresh perspective from my grandfather, the reasons not to at least explore it further no longer seemed so persuasive. In fact, it helped to clarify what I wanted: it wasn't about making an album that sold millions of copies. I just wanted to hear the songs, the bass lines, the harmonies, and the guitar leads the way I heard them in my head. Rationale, I thought, might have to take a backseat. I didn't have a clue where to start.

I spent days crafting an ad to find other musicians, and then days more to put the flyers around town. Weeks went by — no response. Zero. But when old doubts started to creep back, and I thought about moving on, I was energized by some lines in a book I was reading at the time. There was a character in it whose motto was "Two tears in a bucket, motherfuck it..." Elaborating, she said she had learned "not to worry about things that didn't matter." I kept looking.

> "I just wanted to hear the songs the way I heard them in my head."

One night a couple of months later, I went to a small local club to hear some new bands play. I saw three groups perform and one in particular was good. At the bar after their gig, I bumped into their guitarist Greg and congratulated him. Over beers, we got talking about music and ended up exchanging e-mail addresses, vowing to play some day soon. We met up a few weeks later — this time with a couple of guitars. He wanted to hear a few of my songs. I was nervous and played awkwardly at first, but remembering why I was here — "two tears"! — I started to loosen up.

From there, momentum gathered. Greg liked the music. And, importantly, he figured we'd have a good time recording. Having just built a home studio for his own band, Greg offered to record some tracks when he was available. Initially, we were going to record just five songs. But with me having lived with them for so long, we burned through the basic tracks of thirteen songs in two days.

During weekends and any spare time we had, we added more instruments over the next months. The songs began to take shape. They were long, intense days, punctuated with brief coffee breaks. Most of the time I could hardly believe my luck as to where I was and what I was doing. That nine-year-old self was back in the room buzzing with ideas. If we could capture the atmosphere we felt in the room, the mad joy of making something from nothing, then we knew we could make something of worth. Twelve full days of recording later, at a bargain cost of $1,000, I had made an album.

Coming up with the album's title wasn't hard. In homage to the spirit in which it was made, the album was called *Please Yourself*.

When we finished the final mix, I sat back, closed my eyes, and listened to the whole album for the first time. Thirteen songs that had been stuck in my head for years now spilled out in full stereo, filling the room. Relief ran through my bloodstream. My mind, body, and bank account could all fall to pieces, but this couldn't be taken away. I knew, whether or not I lived another five years or another fifty, that "recording an album" was, for me, an experience that I would remember for the rest of my life.

As for my grandfather, he held on for some time after I had last seen him, so we'd continue to speak on the phone (he was in another country) from time to time. By the end, he was really ready to go. Just before he died, though, he heard the songs. I managed to mail him one of the first copies of the finished album. Calling him up one last time, I made sure to tell him how much that afternoon months before had meant. And for the very first time, he told me how proud he was and left me with some parting words: "I didn't know you could sing!"

Watch a ballet · Play in an orchestra · Perform Hamlet in the open air

What's the toughest creative challenge you've ever faced?

If you had to give a speech, what would you choose as your topic?

Do you have a secret you would one day hope to share with someone?

Is there somebody you know who can help you fulfill an artistic ambition of yours?

Name a creative pursuit that you would like to try that might surprise those who know you.

6

FADE TO →

Name something you've failed at that you would like to try again.

What one talent of yours would you most like to receive recognition for?

What contemporary work of art do you think will stand the test of time?

To "Love"...

No.73 PROPOSE

LOVE

Making plans together • Losing track of time • Sharing secrets • Going on a blind date • The raising of eyebrows • Choosing sides of the bed • Missing them when they're not there • Getting down on one knee • Hanging out with friends • Having people over to stay • Offering a shoulder to cry on • Getting the family together • Knowing someone your whole life…

Ask out a total stranger

Karen, 40, San Francisco

I noticed him the first Friday after starting my summer job. I went to the bank to cash my $74 paycheck from the university and there he stood behind Window 2, dressed in a navy blue blazer that outlined his muscular build. His blond hair was thick with a touch of a wave. His gold-plated name plaque said "Mr. Brower."

I stood in line behind a bunch of suits and paint-covered overalls until he called me forward. "Next," he said as he flashed a row of flawless pearly whites. I stared at the brown tile floor as I walked toward him.

I slid my paycheck across the counter while carefully inspecting the intricate design of the chain attached to the pen.

"Can I see some ID?" he asked in a Barry White tone of voice.

I fished in my purse for my wallet as dots of moisture spread across my palms. He scribbled some numbers on the back of my check, opened the cash drawer, and then handed me my money.

"Have a good day," he said as I scurried toward the door.

I looked forward to Fridays. I couldn't wait to go to the bank. What would he be wearing this week? Would he touch my hand when giving me my money? I was ecstatic when he called me by name or asked me about my day. I was devastated when I got summoned to another teller's window.

Each week I dared myself to open up a bit more. "How's it going?" I asked him one afternoon, after practicing for an hour in front of the mirror. "Have any plans for the weekend?" I fished, after two months of lusting.

I started making my co-workers accompany me to the bank so they could interpret his body language as I spoke to him. I talked my extroverted friends into opening accounts at that branch so they could gather information from him. Is he single? How old is he? Does he like me? Friday afternoons, we would huddle at my desk and try to put the pieces together. As best we could tell, he spent weekends with his buddies, he was in his early twenties, and he grinned more around me than the other customers. But he wasn't making any moves.

It was the middle of August and I couldn't stand it anymore. My summer job was winding down and my fantasies were taking over. I had planned our wedding and named our children, but I didn't even know Mr. Brower's first name. I had to ask him out.

I walked into the bank with a withdrawal slip in my hand. It was crumpled from the last two weeks' worth of aborted attempts. This was the day I had to do it.

He was working at the corporate window at the end of the counter. It was just before noon. He looked a bit more frazzled than usual as he handed a customer her brown leather pouch. I took a deep breath and walked up to him before anyone else could cut in.

I didn't say a thing. I just handed him the withdrawal slip. My legs started to quiver and I felt my cheeks fill with heat, but I stood there and watched him read every single word:

DATE: *August 14th*
WITHDRAWAL: *Mr. Brower*
IN THE AMOUNT OF: *One Date*
PAY TO THE ORDER OF: *Karen Myers (me)*
ACCOUNT NUMBER: *215-555-0107 (my phone number)*

His furrowed eyebrows slowly softened and then he laughed. "Wow," he mumbled. Then he looked up at me and smiled.

I smiled back and held his gaze for a moment. Then I strutted out the front door.

He called that night. His first name is John.

 ## Fall in love
Chris, 34, Paris

Her name is Katarzyna and she's Polish. She's also classy, with enough sassiness to make her fun in salsa clubs. She's an intellectual and an adventurer, and she'd be angry if I listed her accomplishments. She has a sparkle that goes well with flowing dresses and exotic scarves in sea breezes. I know of at least three other men who wanted to marry her.

Meet the parents · Spend a night out on the town · Take a bath together

I got to be the lucky one because I was persistent. On our very first date I got lost and ended up panting an apology after running around half of Krakow's old town. She, sitting on a park bench in November, told me she never waited more than 20 minutes. She had waited for me for more than 30 minutes. I made up for it by saying witty things in an art gallery and then buying her coffee. She said witty things back, and we were young. Two dates later I tried to kiss her and she turned away.

Two months of her playing it cool later, I invite her over for dinner and she brings some music she says I should listen to. I cook stir-fry passably and then, candles lit, wine poured, she turns on what she says is Eskimo music from Norway. She got it from a friend. She's like that.

The music comes on and turns out to be a man and a woman singing with no instrumental backup. But they're not singing. They're panting at each other and the back-and-forth builds into a throb of grunts and groans until they explode, sigh, then giggle. By the time the singers had gotten to the building throb, Katarzyna had turned bright red and I had a smile like a Cheshire cat.

Nearly 10 years later, I still do. I know I'm the lucky one.

2DO2DAY

76

Share a fantasy with your partner

Consummate your relationship in an unusual place

Engage in games of exotic role-play

Have a threesome

Smother your lover in honey

Honeymoon in the Galápagos Islands

Caitlin, 31, New York City

It was the wrong man, not the giant lizards, that kept me from the Galápagos Islands the first time. After years of dating, my college boyfriend and I were planning a postgraduation adventure. I could hardly believe what I saw in the guidebooks.

The islands are the most remote on the planet. On a map they are a cluster of tiny dots swimming in the middle of the Pacific Ocean. Before Darwin's famous visit, evil spirits were rumored to inhabit the Galápagos. Bizarre animals—enormous reptiles and land-bound birds—occupied the islands, without any human beings. This arrangement had worked a peculiar magic. When the explorers arrived, the animals were not afraid of them; indeed, they hardly moved when people approached. Even today, the giant tortoises and sea creatures confront travelers with only a sideways glance.

I didn't make it to the islands then. My boyfriend and I made a final split-up and I abandoned the trip. But the Galápagos stayed with me.

Years later, I met Eric. We began dreaming about our honeymoon moments after we got engaged. Before we discussed guests and caterers, we fantasized about the Canadian Rockies and the Italian Alps. Then Eric suggested the Galápagos. I knew that I'd found the right man.

We spent eight days winding around the archipelago on a three-masted sailboat, exploring a world of nature upside down.

The place we discovered was even stranger than the guidebook images. The islands looked like black-and-white photographs. Lava peaks tore out of the water like a colossal natural mistake. As our boat moved through the channels, gray cliffs streaked with guano emerged and then gave way to an eerie shrub-scraped landscape.

The creatures of the Galápagos were just as uncanny as the land. At the islands' edges, iguanas swam and fishing birds dried their flightless wings. Further inland, giant tortoises, the size of small calves, munched on leaves as peacefully as any pet. In the brush, frigatebirds inflated their throat pouches into giant red balloons, while smaller birds— yellow warblers and island finches—searched for seeds oblivious to our presence. In the Galápagos, all humans are tourists.

Renew my wedding vows · Join the mile-high club · Choose "our" song

The last morning of our honeymoon, I woke as the sun beamed through the cabin porthole. Outside the window was one of the smallest pieces of the island chain and one of its most remote, Daphne Major. The rock stood alone in the ocean, a black knot of lava pressed against a pink sky. I drew Eric's arm around me and watched as the sky turned gold and then a brilliant, soft blue.

78 Come out of the closet
Diana, 60, Washington, DC

I wasn't looking for Margo when she crossed my path. But we connected in an instinctive personal joy that I felt had been missing in my life. I remember trying to slow down the excitement I was feeling, knowing the costs would be high.

At the age of 55, I'd been married for thirty-two years. My husband and I had built a nice, comfortable life together that included two fully grown children and a beautiful house. Falling in love with Margo would mean turning my world upside down. It would mean sacrifices and involve venturing into unfamiliar territory. Just as I thought I was settling down for retirement, I found I couldn't let this go.

I had had crushes on a few women over the years, but nothing had ever happened before. My love life worked, or so I thought. I had always made friends easily and I think I had fooled myself into being something that perhaps I wasn't. I had never felt this way before. My God, I thought, I was a lesbian. No wonder making future plans had been so difficult. I had been playing parts.

I told my husband. It was the most difficult decision of my life, and yet the most liberating. I liked the person I was becoming. Every day was a revelation to me. The feeling of relief, that this was where I was meant to go, was so profound. My self-respect was growing and I knew I wanted to spend the last part of my life with Margo.

It's now been five years. I still live in the same city, but now in a small apartment with Margo. My two grown children remain my deep-seated loves and they return that love with an understanding I never thought possible. We speak on an almost daily basis and they seem to like the mother they have now even more than before. She comes with laughter, with support, and, best of all, free of anger and regret.

There are painful reminders of my old life that occasionally hurt. I have lost a few of the friendships of my old "couple" friends. And some invitations have stopped coming. At the same time, the majority of my relationships have strengthened. I have reconnected with friends I had lost touch with and have made a host of new friends I treasure.

Recently, one friend quietly told me she almost did what I did, but in the end, lacked the will to make such a change. Still another acquaintance said I gave our older generation hope that love could be found late in life.

In the end, my goal had been simple: I wanted to be honest. I wanted to trust not only my partner but myself. Though it meant losing the nice house and the invitations that went with a comfortable lifestyle, I have no regrets. Things I thought were important before pale in significance. Not long ago, a good friend sent me W. H. Auden's poem "Leap Before You Look." That's what *I* did. Knowing how time can catch you up, I made the leap. The funny thing is, I feel more like a woman now than I ever felt before.

Hide away for the weekend   -   Write letters to my friends more often

Start a family
Christopher, 32, Berkeley, CA

My wife and I had been talking about having a baby for years. So, in a way, you could say the conception of our firstborn was more than simply sperm meets egg. In fact, we'd been talking about having a child for as long as we'd been together. It's not that we didn't make progress on the child concept. We talked about our hypothetical child often. We talked about religion, schools, and discipline. We even thought about names — one for a boy and one for a girl. That took up about seven of our eight years of marriage.

Finally we went for it. The gloves came off, so to speak. And given our propensity to talk this thing to death, we were ready. We had the thermometer and the little tabs to detect ovulation. We would try at different times of the day and at varying times of the month leading up to the optimal time (and after). Alas, a few months passed and even though everyone we know spent a year or more trying before being successful, we were sure we'd have gotten it right already.

As it turns out, all that time you spend worrying about getting pregnant when you're a teenager is based on some incomplete information. It doesn't always happen. In fact, it can be really hard to get pregnant. A lot of things have to be perfect for the conception to occur. It's like hitting a home run in baseball. Even if you get the perfect pitch in the perfect part of the strike zone, you still have to put the perfect swing on the ball.

It took about four or five months, I guess. In fact, we had sort of written off the current month for the purposes of conceiving. My wife was ill and we were certain that we'd missed our window. We started to think we were timing the whole thing wrong. And that's when I started to figure this whole child thing out. Whatever you think is going to happen will actually be opposite to the eventual course of events. My wife's next cycle never came.

As I write now, we're halfway there. Four more months and we'll finally get to meet her. Her. We found out this week it's a girl. And now that we know, that name we'd settled on doesn't seem as solid. We've decided to meet her first, and then decide what fits.

Sew my own wedding dress - Teach my son to shave - Call my parents

Give birth

Susie, 33, New York City

Nine months and two days after my wedding, I was in a taxi heading down New York's First Avenue on the way to a hospital to give birth to our first daughter, Sophie.

I had woken up at midnight with the first signs of contractions and wondered whether this really was it or whether it was the repercussions of an Indian meal the night before. As the contractions moved toward the key 5-1-1 pattern (every five minutes, lasting for a minute, for a period of an hour), I realized that our honeymoon baby was definitely on the way, on her due date itself.

I arrived at the hospital and was quickly rigged up to various monitors and was assessed to be a "keeper." My contractions were deemed painful enough for me to be admitted and I was soon lying in the delivery room. Even after months of morning sickness, swollen ankles, and carrying around a huge belly, what was about to happen still didn't seem real. I focused on the blankets and tiny woolly hat at the end of the bed. The hat, which would soon be on my baby's head, seemed to have been placed strategically to help me see beyond the thirteen hours of swearing, screaming, and clinging to my husband Michael's hand that followed. Thank God for epidurals.

Seeing little Sophie for the first time was truly incredible. She turned out to be not so little — nine pounds and nine ounces — and, though bright red and screaming, she was, of course, beautiful and perfect in every way. I felt so many overwhelming emotions and a huge and immediate sense of responsibility and protectiveness toward her. My husband and I were left to spend our first hour as a family alone. We didn't take our eyes off our little swaddled bundle for a moment.

Almost six weeks on, I can't imagine life without Sophie. I am falling more and more in love with her each day and have never felt happier. Yes, my life has changed. The learning curve has been steep and the responsibility sometimes overwhelming, but I will never forget that first smile. Her birth has been the biggest achievement of my life.

Move closer to my family · Watch my kid perform in the school concert

Get married

Tom, 28, London

We weren't the first people to get married. In fact, it's one of the least original things one can ever do, right up there with having kids and a midlife crisis.

I proposed to Tess on holiday in India whilst in the back of a motorized rickshaw. It was an easy decision; we had been with each other for nine years, sharing a home for five, and we never doubted that we would spend our final years together, fighting over the same cup of cocoa. It sounded odd to still refer to Tess as my girlfriend, or even worse, my partner (as if our relationship were some kind of entrepreneurial start-up), and I looked forward to calling her my wife. Besides, despite being a liberal-minded, modern man, the thought of raising a family of little bastards still struck me as somehow inappropriate.

Even at that early stage, I was desperate that the wedding day itself wouldn't be packaged and predictable — just another white wedding to add to the list. For a memoir-obsessed, armchair eccentric like me, it was important to make the day as unique as we could. After all, you don't get another chance to put on a show like this until your funeral.

Within moments of hearing the word "yes," I was in animated discussions with Tess about what kind of wedding we could have. The possibilities were endless. We scribbled down a guest list, drew up fantastic designs of outfits and decorations we hoped to have, and had the idea of a rustic, open-air banquet. For a moment, we even discussed a system of pulleys whereby each guest could be winched up above the gathering to speak as the spirit moved them.

Since I was a lapsed Christian and Tess was as heathen as a summer solstice, there was unholy talk of a pagan ceremony in the woods, along with fantasies of reclaiming a dilapidated barn for an impromptu hoedown. Our favorite idea was to have an Indian-style wedding — Tess and I on horseback, swathed in garlands of flowers and surrounded by the vivid colors of an Indian sunset.

Once back from our holiday, however, we fell to earth with a bump. Very quickly we found that venues, caterers, and even DJs were booked months, sometimes years, in advance. Some people, it seemed, had chosen their caterer at birth.

The cost was also a problem. Every place we saw was hugely expensive, and often came as part of a whole package: caterers, wine, even the tables and chairs. The more these options were limited for us, the less we felt we would be able to leave our own stamp on the day. Anxious we would have to settle for something less personal, we became completely indecisive and our planning reached something of a dead end.

Then, three months on from the proposal, a friend mentioned a house in the heart of the countryside that was available for hire. It didn't come packaged with a dozen extras and offered us the freedom to do everything else the way we wanted to. As we visited the house for the first time and soaked up the beautiful setting, it became apparent that we didn't need to get hitched on board a submarine or swap vows at the top of the Eiffel Tower to create something unique and personal.

Instead, once we had agreed on the venue, we were able to focus on the smaller details to make the day as personal as we could. We picked out flowers, chose the caterers, and spent lazy afternoons testing out a variety of wines. For the ceremony itself, we wrote our own vows, chose some Bollywood music to greet the bride's arrival, and booked the only rickshaw for miles around to whisk us off at the end of the night.

We were able to take control in other homespun ways too. We designed and illustrated the wedding invitations ourselves and made Polaroid place cards for the reception. We also recruited friends to take the photographs and video and to DJ the evening's music.

When the big day finally arrived, the decisions of the past few months came together, and it all sped by at a dreamlike pace. But what made the day truly memorable turned out to be the very first thing we had agreed back in our hotel room in India: the friends and family we had invited as our guests. For all the personal touches we were able to add that April afternoon, ultimately the people we were surrounded by were all we *really* needed to relax, be ourselves, and have as personal and enjoyable a wedding as we could have possibly imagined.

FRIENDS

What's the best party a friend of yours has ever thrown?

If you were getting hitched, who would you pick as your maid of honor/best man?

If all the friends you've ever had gathered in one room, which ones would get on best/worst?

Name someone you've lost contact with in the past five years whom you'd like to call today.

Which of your friends makes you laugh the most?

What's on

LO

SEX

What's the best sex you've ever had?

Name a fantasy you would like to explore with your partner.

Name an unusual place where you would like to "get it on."

What's the most embarrassing episode in your sexual career?

When did you first come to terms with "the facts of life"?

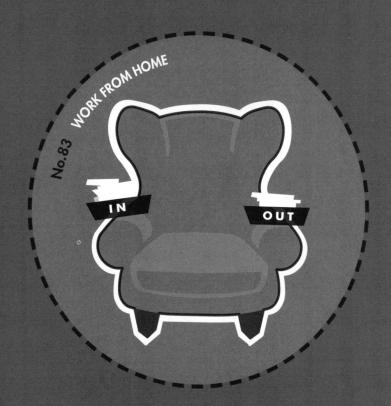

No.83   WORK FROM HOME

IN

OUT

WORK

Getting hired ● Setting the alarm clock ● Building a business ● Brainstorming ideas ● Working with a team ● Figuring out the budget ● Taking pride ● Taking a break ● Working late ● Brewing cups of coffee ● Cashing your paycheck ● Paying the rent ● Going out for drinks ● Gossiping at the water cooler ● Experiencing technical difficulties ● Getting promoted ● Meeting a deadline...

Change my career

Shaun, 36, London

OK, so you get to age thirty-one, you're a single happy-go-lucky-ish bachelor without too many cares in the world, or a proper job (or at least no finely worked-out career path, like most of your seemingly well-adjusted married-with-kids peers), or much money, and suddenly…POW!…you wake up one fine morning to find that you're actually miserably lonely, aimless, penniless, and, quite frankly, a mess.

When I limped out of full-time education age 21, I was so green. It brings a blush to my cheeks just thinking about it. I was only just beginning to become politicized about the world around me, but I was firmly committed to the ideal of doing good, of having a positive and lasting influence on this world, even though I had only the vaguest idea what the world was about.

So for nearly ten years I worked in the charity sector, for a series of charities involved with fair trade, the environment, disabled children, and breast cancer. All the time I was jumping from job to job, from fund raiser to events organizer to personal assistant.

Suddenly, almost a decade of my life had passed by! And although I'm proud of the work that I did in those ten years, there was virtually nothing left for me at the end of it. I had been lurching from one type of job to another, not developing any kind of career, not earning very much money, and working without any kind of security net.

> "I hadn't lived up to anywhere near my potential."

Don't get me wrong; I was enjoying myself. I had many friends, and loved and laughed (and drank) my way through pretty much this whole period of my life. But at thirty-one, I came to the conclusion that I was failing in my career. I hadn't lived up to anywhere near my potential. I was lazy and disorganized and, worse, so much worse than these, I wasn't being truthful to myself, my core nature.

I think I went through a semicontrolled breakdown that year, striving to connect with what I was essentially all about. I spent a painful time trying to dig into my own psyche to find that buried seam of hope and inspiration that could lead me on to great things, or at least back to a

Start a family business - Patent an invention - Train to be a fire jumper

place where I could feel stability, balance, and confidence in the rightness of my determination and choices.

I found what I was looking for by looking back. I had known from an early age that I had a talent for art. I was forever making things in those early years, from paper collages to toys to flamboyant outfits for dressing up. At age twelve, on returning from my first animation festival, I had even cajoled my father into making a lightbox with me so that I could start creating my first animated spectacular on the sheets of cel acetate that I'd saved up for.

Somehow, I had forgotten all of this. I had been tempered by the thoughts and opinions of others around me to the extent that I no longer believed that being artistically creative could play anything but a backseat role in my future.

What I came out with from this experience was very simply this: that I would inevitably become a husk so riven with anger and regrets that I would spend the rest of my life devoid of any joy or fulfillment. OK, so slightly melodramatic, but that's the earnest, beleaguered mind-set that giving yourself a good kicking for twelve months can place you in! It was at this point that I decided that it was high time to convert all this angst into action; I needed to go back to school!

Miraculously, within three months of making that crucial decision (and with more than a little help from my parents) I had embarked upon a highly vocational and intensive six-month animation course, learning traditional skills at a local college.

It sounds slightly tyrannical, an edge of megalomania creeping in. But to be able to create and sustain life across a handful of pieces of paper produced the utmost feeling of joy in me. I could animate! I felt great satisfaction in bringing shape and form to my thought patterns with pencil and paper, and making them dance — well OK, not dance, but I'd at least got them doing very stilted, jittery walk cycles! I thought it was something I could build on.

With these new skills, I was able to draw upon the friends and contacts that I'd built up within the charity sector the previous decade and forge a fresh start. It was a mammoth exercise, requiring a terrific amount of hard work and persistence, but gradually, over the past five years, I've managed to get a fairly steady stream of work producing educational animations for the Internet that serve to promote good causes to new audiences.

I've found myself a career path, a collision of creative passion and idealistic zeal, that might (hope upon hope) eventually lead to the type of fluid brand of security that I could live with. I still feel underpaid and undervalued on occasion, and the stress of deadlines is still very real, but I'm much happier. I now know I have a talent to sell and a skill to practice that can be applied to those very causes that I'd felt so very passionately about in my twenties.

85 Be a schoolteacher
SuzAnne, 62, Houston

Driving past the college where I used to teach, I notice cars flooding into already too-full parking lots, and suddenly, inexplicably, sadness floods me. Instructors are preparing lesson plans and lectures; students are shopping for books and binders and worrying about schedules. School bells are ringing again — but not for me. By choice, I am no longer part of this scene.

It's been almost six years since I last taught at Houston Community College. I thought then that I was just taking a break to finish a book. However, the interruption has become permanent. My husband has retired, and I've realized that to be free to write and to travel with him, I will probably never again stand in front of a class.

It's a sensible choice, I tell myself, remembering what I never liked about teaching. When I was in school in the fifties, girls considered only

Pay off my loans - Become a physical therapist - Be my own boss

three occupations — secretary, nurse, teacher. Since I couldn't master the hooks and wiggles of shorthand and was not particularly brave about blood, teaching it became. I chose English because it was easy — and because I admired Madge Gibson, my senior English teacher, called "Mighty Madge" outside the classroom, both a jest at her four-feet, ten-inch height and a tribute to her power over hormone-addled seniors.

My teaching career began when I was twenty. As a student, I taught a summer session of recalcitrant students, most of whom had failed English the previous year. By the end of the course, I questioned the wisdom of my career choice, but I had no alternatives. At twenty-two, newly married, a substitute teacher in a rough high school, I was so naïve my students locked me out of the classroom.

Seldom as a substitute did I get to teach the literature I loved; usually I found myself teaching remedial grammar — and sometimes gym. "That's not my field," I would protest. "That's okay," a cheery voice would respond. "You're young enough to keep up. Wear pants and be on campus in thirty minutes."

So I went back to university for a junior college teaching credential; when our sons were in preschool and kindergarten, I started teaching at the community college, where opportunities to teach literature expanded and discipline was easier. But still there were problems: students who loudly complained when they received the grades they earned rather than those they fantasized; students who didn't believe that writing clear, coherent essays or reading literary masterpieces was important.

"I questioned the wisdom of my career choice, but I had no alternatives."

Grading exams, daily work, and six to ten essays per student each semester, plus reading their journals, absorbed time I'd rather have spent with my family. Classes were usually too large to offer the individual attention some students needed. Administrative paperwork and committee responsibilities consumed more time, time better spent preparing lectures or reading professional journals. My salary was meager. Some classrooms were barely adequate — overcrowded, freezing or steaming, poorly lit. And I never had an office. Instead, the trunk of my car became my mobile desk; a cardboard box, my file cabinet.

And yet I also remember the joys of teaching. The first day of class, rows of unfamiliar faces, knowing what I wanted to teach, wondering what I would learn, eager for our mutual adventure to begin. On some days insights crackled, and we became a learning community.

My admiration and respect for some of the men and women I taught over the years is boundless; I only hope I conveyed that regard to them. Blue-collar workers adapted to new technology so they could keep their families housed and fed. High school rebels and dropouts, realizing nothing good would ever happen unless they made it happen, obtained GEDs and enrolled in college. Older women, children raised, husbands occupied, decided it was their turn. They came, nervous and insecure; to witness them discovering their capacity for learning and growth was an honor. Foreign students dared to obtain college degrees while still maintaining their own culture. To teach these students, to channel their longing, resentment, hope, and anxiety into written expression that satisfied convention without sacrificing distinctive voices, was a pleasure.

I miss them and I miss my colleagues — celebrating each other's triumphs and honors; sharing teaching techniques; attending state, regional, and national conferences; even the banter in the workroom as we cursed the photocopy machine.

The sight of school starting will always make me feel restless and out of sorts. I can only remember that, in one way or another, all of us teach. We teach others by living our lives as authentically as we can. Perhaps it is no more possible to retire from teaching than it is to retire from life.

Teach in Japan for a year - Open a flower shop - Host a radio show

86 Take a new route to work

If you normally walk, see what you're missing and drive a car. If you feel guilty about your emissions, take a scenic stroll to your workstation.

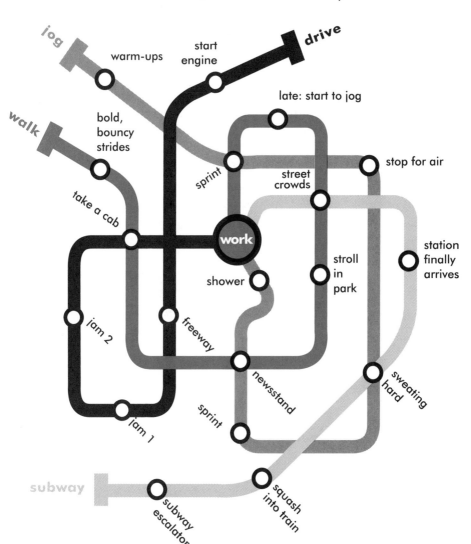

Run a bed and breakfast

Ana Maria, 56, Salem, OR

The first time I saw Leadville, the snow fell gently on its unpaved side streets. The 1890s homes blanketed in white snow made me feel like I had stepped back a century or so. I wished I could live there.

Years later, when my husband found a job in Leadville, we moved with our four-year-old daughter. The town was booming with the Climax mine open. In a town with 2,000 workers, 1,500 jobs were provided by the mine. There were no apartments available and no vacant houses.

We settled in a room at the Delaware Hotel that first evening. When night came, we could hear people having fun on the streets and at a bar across the way. At midnight, we were awakened by someone running after another person through the hotel corridors and actually shooting a gun. I felt we were living in the set for *Bonanza*.

We were desperate to get out of the hotel, and searched all possibilities for housing. Our meager savings were not enough to buy a house, but we still looked. We came across a large house and we explained we just wanted to look at it, but did not have enough money to buy it.

After the grand tour, we were surprised to hear the owner say he wanted to work with us to get us the house. He came up with a plan that would involve us living downstairs while we would rent the house to miners. Our income could not pay for the mortgage, so that meant we had to make it work from the first month. If anything went wrong, we would not have a way to meet emergencies. But we were young and I have always been a bit of a dreamer, so we went ahead and bought the house.

"We needed to do something to rescue our house."

For a year and a half all went well. I was able to stay home and be with my daughter and still have a life of my own.

It was then that the town's employer, the big reliable mine, started to close. Lots of people lost their homes and lots of businesses went broke. We lost our tenants and it looked like the end.

We needed to do something to rescue our house. We had saved a little during that year of renting rooms, and we decided to invest the money in antiques and opening up a bed and breakfast.

We were lucky because the house we had bought had been a governor's home at the turn of the century. It was a great platform to present skits and give history tours. We'd invite the town's elders to tell history as they remembered it, and later we would contrast what they had said with pieces of history we would read aloud.

There were times when we had a pianist living with us and he would play, and my husband, children, and guests would sing along. It was a great opportunity for visitors to get acquainted with the townspeople and experience their culture firsthand. They were vibrant, exhilarating times.

Thirteen years later, we had to leave Leadville. But the remembrance of our life there is of a time when we led a storybook life in a storybook town.

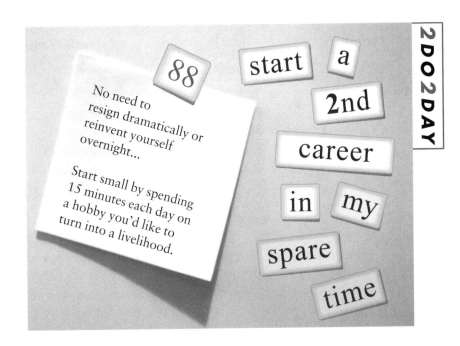

88

No need to resign dramatically or reinvent yourself overnight...

Start small by spending 15 minutes each day on a hobby you'd like to turn into a livelihood.

2 DO 2 DAY

start a 2nd career in my spare time

Enter the priesthood - Pass my law exams - Become a shepherd

89 Open a restaurant

James, 30, London

I had been working as an actor for five years, with a good deal of "resting" in between roles. To make ends meet, I had to rely on other work, and I was getting tired of it involving things that didn't stretch me in any way. Dressing up in banana suits, amongst other of my jobs, wasn't where I wanted to be in my thirties.

I had spent time studying café-theater in Paris. One thought led to another, and the idea of doing something aside from acting and waiting for work emerged. Restaurants and bars have so many similar traits to acting, especially the theater, and I began to think up a concept for a restaurant that had a very warm and welcoming feel, a delicious menu, and an area set aside for performing plays, poetry, and music.

One evening about four years ago, fueled by a little too much wine, I finally told a few friends of what I hoped to do. I decided the more people who knew, the more likely I would take action, as pride would eventually play a part. Whatever happened, I would have to see it to the end.

Reality soon set in. Having spent my 20s fitting in jobs, I hadn't gathered a great deal of gritty business experience en route. Business plans, forecasts, site viewings, building control, local authorities didn't really feature on my résumé. The learning curve grew steeper and steeper. Not to mention the fact that, at that time, my only experience in catering was as an 18-year-old barman.

Mainly, I learned as I went along. I eventually found work as a manager in a couple of restaurants, where I began to learn how to work with the chefs — notoriously sensitive to handle! And I began to look at what felt like an endless number of sites in and around the city. I came very close to signing a couple.

Then I came across an old toy shop where I used to buy my train sets as a kid. It had recently been totally gutted. I thought we could make it work.

From that moment on, things happened very fast. I did my best to squeeze money out of friends and family who had agreed to help

Work as a freelance consultant - Sell vintage cars for a living - Train horses

support this venture. The fact that I had put my own life on hold to throw everything I had at it convinced them of how serious I was. Even then, quite a few people backed out when it came to actually signing the check, and those who did sign did so in full knowledge that they could lose it all.

Perhaps understandably, not enough money was raised to hire a full crew to renovate the site. In order to open the restaurant, I would have to be completely hands-on throughout the building and fit-out. With great help from my girlfriend, family, and friends, who acted as gofers, painters, and everything in between, the renovation took about five months. It was probably the most satisfying part of the entire process.

"What kept me motivated? Blind faith played a part."

Construction work slowly transformed into sourcing food, selecting wines, hiring staff, designing the logo, and countless other things. Then, the pinnacle — seeing our chef cook for our very first customers. Alchemy Bar & Restaurant was born.

It was very exciting. Serving the first customer who wasn't family or a friend felt surreal. Only the night before, at 2 a.m., I had been typing out the menu in the restaurant while my girlfriend, brother, and a friend were putting the final touches to decorating the basement. We literally didn't have a moment to draw breath. It almost felt like the first customers were intruders into our building site.

Plus, as the renovations had taken up all of my time, it had been almost six months since I had managed a restaurant. So when customers arrived, I had to wipe the plasterboard off my face, pick the paint out of my fingernails, and don the crisp shirt to prepare to serve gourmet food to our first customers.

What kept me motivated? Blind faith played a part. I'm quite stubborn too, and I like a project. Seeing a dream slowly become reality, and having to work very hard for that reality to happen, was quite fantastic.

Looking back, I was certainly a little naive to think that experience could be had on the job. A proprietor has to know everything about everything. I am a good cook at home, but it's another skill altogether in a commercial kitchen. That's one area I have to dive deeper into in the future.

I am now fifteen months down the line. Doing your own thing, so to speak, is very rewarding, but, at this early stage at least, it is relentless. Running a restaurant is all-consuming. Daily triumphs and pleasures are constantly tempered with trials and problems. There is always a problem round the corner. That's one thing I've learned.

I can't see myself treading any boards other than those at the restaurant for some time to come, but then, at the moment, I wouldn't have it any other way.

Quit my job
Daniel, 29, New York City

Put the word *investment* in front of the term *bankers' hours,* and you mutate the euphemism to mean not a short workday but the sweat-producing, spirit-reducing, ulcer-inducing hours between 7 a.m. and 11 p.m.

For two years I worked those hours, six — sometimes seven — days a week. The exhaustion every evening was only eclipsed by the fatigue of the following morning. Outside the office, what I saw of mornings and evenings was distinguishable only by subtly different shades of black. Their darkness flowed out of and into my nightmarish sleep.

But as morbid as those few personal hours were, at least they hinted at some taste of freedom. Office hours, on the other hand, suggested freedom was just an illusion. In blinding contrast to the natural darkness associated with home, the office immersed me in the flickering world of fluorescent lighting and flashing monitors. The artificial brightness only emphasized my chosen lifestyle's shadowy nature.

"There was the promise of one day living like the boss."

Each day I plodded through my shifting routine, a quicksand of conference calls, spreadsheets, and analyst reports; treacherous enough to prohibit autopiloting but never quite interesting enough to generate a spike in brain activity. A vampire navigating a cubicle graveyard, I hunted my only luxury — not blood, but the energy rush of a Venti Iced Mocha-Chino Blast. With no Starbucks in the building, these also provided my only exposure to natural light during the daytime.

So why did I bother?

The answer wasn't very complicated: I simply didn't know any better. This job, or at least the Hollywood version of it, was everything I wanted from life. As a kid, finance fascinated me. My hero: Alex Keaton from *Family Ties*. My favorite movie: *Wall Street*. I didn't have Kathy Ireland or a Lamborghini posted above my bed, but Gordon Gecko's speech, "Greed Is Good." I made my first investment when I was eight — $250 saved from two birthdays — in International Thoroughbred Breeders no less. A bet on betting. My current library still consists largely of books by all the usual suspects — Lefèvre, Graham, Fisher — a cemetery I don't have the courage to exhume even now. I read *Liar's Poker* three times.

"Someday," I thought, "I'll be a big swinging dick."

So the real question is not why did I go into investment banking, but why did I stay? I'd be lying if I said the adrenaline, the attention, and the

growing bank account I never had the time to enjoy weren't all contributors. There was a certain allure to the limousines, private concerts with Broadway stars, and first-row seats at the Victoria's Secret runway show.

In addition, there was the promise of one day living like the boss: hosting lavish parties at an actual castle in the Hamptons; taking last-minute junkets to St. Barths; arriving midfield, midgame to little Jesse's soccer championship in a private helicopter.

"I don't know which punch pushed me over the edge."

But subconsciously, I suspected that all of it was not worth the years I was throwing away; and eventually, I learned that the castles, the Caribbean, and the copters were not the whole story. You don't hear about the boss's sleeping bag under the desk during earnings season, you don't hear about his high blood pressure or stress-induced irritable bowel disease. Unless you know him well, you don't hear him comment that, up close, you can see the cellulite on a supermodel's thighs. My media collection rarely portrayed these back alleys of Wall Street, and I discovered too late that if you want to know what lifelong success at your job will deliver, you just have to look at the lifestyles of those in charge.

So why did I stay?

That was also not very complicated. Fear. Fear of the alternatives. Fear of the unknown. Fear of failure. When you've spent your entire life pursuing a dream that turns out to be a nightmare, what do you do next?

A bad job is like a bad relationship and, like a battered husband, chances were I wouldn't realize how terrible my job was until I got out. Then there was the possibility I was the problem — maybe I was a masochist, maybe I needed to be browbeaten on a regular basis. Even if I did manage to quit, I might just plunge into the open arms of another bad relationship.

I knew all this. I also knew that with every passing day the likelihood of a successful escape diminished. I don't know which punch pushed me over the edge. It could have been the night I worked until 6 a.m. constructing the Exodus earnings model. I bumped into the boss on my way out — he had arrived an hour early for the 7 a.m. sales call. "Don't be late," he said.

Or maybe it was the time I reviewed my bank statement and realized I had paid $1,200 for a gym membership I hadn't used in a year. I snuck out early one day, not so much to improve my health as to reduce my per session charge to a more acceptable $600. When I got to the gym, I found myself the proud owner of an additional 20 pounds and 20 heartbeats per minute. That's $3 per pound-beat, a ratio that could make the best analyst tremble.

Or maybe it was the time that, with construction just begun on his six-figure office fireplace, the boss explained the impact of cost cuts on my bonus.

But whatever the reason was, on a certain summer day, I walked into his office. With the brand-new fireplace crackling next to us, I explained that I wouldn't be there for the morning sales call; and, no, I wouldn't be dialing in.

I stroll past the row of black limousines suffering under the same sunrays that now nourish my skin. It's five miles home, but I can't imagine not walking. It will take a while for my body to adjust to my new lifestyle, even longer for my mind. But I'm thrilled to initiate that process. As I take a deep swig of the 35¢ deli coffee that soothes me more that the $4.65 Mocha-Chino Blast ever did, I realize that once in a while walking away from something is the courageous thing to do.

Rewrite my CV - Refuse a lucrative opportunity on the basis of principles

The Career Path

- WORK -

What was the first job you ever had?

If every job paid exactly the same, what would you choose to do?

- A shrewd investment -

If you worked from home, what would you miss about the office?

Name a job you would do for free.

Who do you most like working with?

Name the proudest achievement of your career so far.

Honesty rewarded

What's the worst job you've ever had?

What's the longest you've gone without employment?

What skills of yours do you think are most underutilized?

PENCILS

- An enterprising initiative -

If you could dedicate half a day each week to different work, what would it be?

How much money do you need to live comfortably?

What's the luckiest break of your career so far?

Name a friend whose career you envy.

What job would you most like to have 10 years from now?

What profession is the most undervalued? Overvalued?

Have you ever had a business idea you felt could genuinely work?

- A successful interview -

To "Legacy"...

What did you want to be when you were eight? How far did you get?

How many hours a week do you work?

What's your definition of "success"?

No.91

BURY TREASURE

LEGACY

Leaving something behind after you're gone ● Helping the next generation ● Growing old ● Giving it all away ● Making your mark ● Paying respects to those who have come before ● Passing stories on ● Recalling triumphs ● Stewing over regrets ● Keeping traditions alive ● Sharing wisdom ● Inspiring others ● Looking back at what you've done ● Remembering old friends ● Saying goodbye...

92 Continue a family tradition

Eric, 32, Providence, RI

My great-grandfather was a Norwegian Lutheran missionary in Fort Dauphin, Madagascar. In the year 1900, he carved his name in script on a rock atop the island's highest peak, overlooking the Indian Ocean.

His son — my grandfather — also became a missionary in Madagascar, and in the year 1933 he carved his name on the same rock, just below my great-grandfather's.

My own father was born and raised in Madagascar, but he never returned. After he died, I went on to college and then medical school.

Three years ago, I volunteered for a rotation at the missionary hospital outside Fort Dauphin, and one weekend my sister and I made the climb to the top of Pic St. Louis to see our great-grandfather's stone. The carved names were there, and the view was incredible. A week later, I hiked up alone with hammer and chisel, and carved my father's initials and mine just below Grandpa's.

There is not a drop of Malagasy blood in my body, but that place is the most rooted place for me on earth. I have an old photograph on my wall of my great-grandfather hiking down the path from the top of Pic St. Louis. He is looking back at the camera, and I now know just how he felt.

Watch my son grow up
Neil, 36, London

I looked on as my sixteen-month-old son, Peter, got the first haircut of his life. The fact that he was sitting in the exact same chair as I had for my own haircut just a couple of weeks before only served to highlight the transformation that had taken place in both our lives over the last year and a half.

Peter's hair had remained wild, unruly, and uncut up to this point. As his locks fell to the floor, part of me was amazed we'd made it this far. During those Laurel and Hardy first days of parenthood, Lisa and I had at times felt as helpless as our baby, rushing around like the couple of beginners we truly were. Just as it is for all new parents, nothing could have prepared us for the day when we brought Peter home from hospital. Our old lives were gone forever.

Of course, Peter was blissfully unaware of any of the significance I was attaching to his first haircut. He happily played with a shampoo bottle while swaying his head this way and that in an effort to evade the hairdresser's persistent hands. Luckily, he seemed to find her only mildly irritating, so there were no tears or tantrums, just a little bewilderment.

Since those early days, Peter has changed beyond all recognition. From being absolutely helpless, immobile, and new to the world, he now walks (if a little drunkenly), says some words and short sentences, eats with a spoon, climbs the stairs, splashes in the bath, plays with his friends, flirts with waitresses, and, most important, laughs at my jokes.

"Part of me was amazed we'd made it this far."

But why did this, my son's first haircut, feel so very significant to me? At the center of the massive change that had occurred in my life and his was a revolutionary change in the whole order of things. I was no longer identified just as Lisa's partner, or my dad's son. I'm Peter's dad. He depends on me, learns from me, is amused (sometimes tickled pink) by me. I am his big invincible dad. With these thoughts came a totally different perspective on the life of my own dad. It struck me that he must

Have an obituary headline in the paper - Start my memoirs - Write a will

have struggled too. I felt certain that there must have been many times when he, like me now, felt far from invincible. But as I was growing up, invincible was how I had seen my dad all the same.

After Peter's haircut, we took some locks of my son's hair and put them in a little bag as a memento for ourselves, and to pass on to his grandparents.

Peter's face had transformed over the course of his haircut. He really looked different: smarter, more mature. As I pushed the pram through the hairdresser's door out into the warm sunshine and looked down at his beaming face, I sensed we had entered a fresh new stage of our lives. Both of us somehow seemed a little older: Peter looking it, and me feeling it. What lay ahead, who knew! But I knew I would always remember this moment.

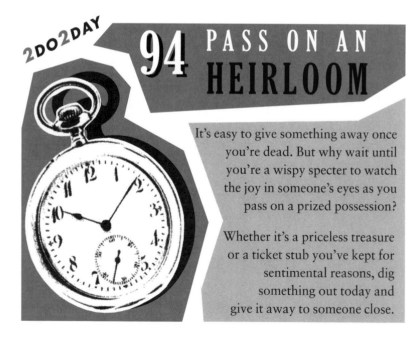

2DO2DAY

94 PASS ON AN HEIRLOOM

It's easy to give something away once you're dead. But why wait until you're a wispy specter to watch the joy in someone's eyes as you pass on a prized possession?

Whether it's a priceless treasure or a ticket stub you've kept for sentimental reasons, dig something out today and give it away to someone close.

Give away all of my possessions - *Receive an honorary degree*

95 Plant a tree

Colin, 72, Letchworth, England

When George VI was crowned king in 1937, it was decided to mark the occasion by having a large number of young schoolchildren troop to the local park to plant an avenue of horse chestnut trees.

We were smartly dressed, not in gardening attire, and I can distinctly remember as a six-year-old being handed a small shovel and being told to heap some earth around the base of the tree.

We were told that the secret of a successful planting is to tread the roots in well, and, as I recall, our teacher singled out the fattest lad present, Tubby Williams, whose large boots sank deep in the earth as he dutifully padded around the new tree.

Nearly seventy years later, it's a sobering thought that I am older than the huge, healthy horse chestnut tree that I helped plant when it was just a sapling. I have lived within a few hundred yards from the park all these years, so it has been easy to keep an eye on "my tree" and monitor its progress. Now a towering giant around ninety feet high and with a three-foot-diameter trunk, the tree has given me a lifetime of pleasure.

96 Follow in my mom's footsteps

Bruce, 46, Indianapolis

Standing at the edge of Mom's open grave, I felt something profound, focusing, existential, that led to an unexpected commitment: I'm gonna do it like she did it.

This was a surprising moment. The grave is in Indianapolis, where I grew up, and, like many, many others, I had left Indianapolis almost as soon as I could to find a bigger and more exciting world.

Growing up in the suburbs there, I simply assumed that my parents were content. We took some trips, to New York, to L.A., to Montreal, but we were always "glad to be home."

My first clue otherwise should have been that my mom was not a particularly good mom, not in the way that all parents can fail or frustrate their children, but in a manner of basic orientation. As a teenager, I could not know that there are source waters to the unhappiness of adults; as her son, I could not care.

And be like her? No.

When I moved away, to the East Coast, our relationship began to right itself slowly. At some point, in a phone call, she let me know that she wondered if I'd be willing to meet her and Dad at JFK Airport to say hello and grab a bite as they changed planes on their way to Tibet.

Tibet.

She couched the trip in the safety of a group trip from her church, where ten or twelve of them had decided to see firsthand some of the work of a mission outreach there. My born-on-a-farm father was not particularly interested in going, but, she said, you don't get many chances to do something like this. And off they went.

Some years later, another phone conversation: If you call and we're not here, it's because we're going to visit a remarkable outreach to street children and orphanages in Romania. Upon their return, I heard stories of Mom being helped to descend into the sewers, to see for herself homeless children living there in squalor.

Her health began a long, slow deterioration, as some very central systems began to fail: diabetes, kidney problems. In the same call that I tried to find out the status of some of these things, she informed me that she had an invitation from one of her pastors to accompany him and his adopted child back to his homeland in South Africa. And Dad didn't want to go this time, so Dad wasn't going.

This time, things were not so smooth, as I learned when Dad called to tell me she was coming home early, alone, because of a somewhat severe stomach virus. After I hung up, I calculated the hours she would be sitting on an airplane, over the ocean, fighting off a disabling and humiliating condition. And I knew that I would hear only a brief paragraph about that before being shown the pictures and videos, and hearing the stories about soccer games and monkeys in the trees.

After her own mother died, it became slowly clearer to my sister and me that our mother was someone who had been discontent probably from the get-go. An only child of Depression-era parents, she must have experienced her life as a set of shackles that had no key. Marrying and staying in Indianapolis, however imprisoning, felt like her only option; having children, for her, locked all the remaining exits.

It's easy to say that, when she finally could, she simply fled the coop. Almost as a final act of revenge on everyone, she was financing these trips with her parents' estate, money she refused to share with Dad unless he went along.

But there was more going on than that. Her trips in her waning years, arguably unwise, were a declaration of what mattered to her, of at last being able to indulge her boundless interest in things that could not ever be found in Indianapolis. You go places, whether well or infirm, because they are there, and because there is something about yourself that you will not learn if you sit still. She went to visit ministries to orphans, but the orphans were ministering right back to her.

How easy, at her graveside, to recall all that I had never received from my mother. Some of the only tangibles I had left were photos of her trips, torn boarding passes, and toiletry kits from US Airways. But, whether I chose to value them or not, these would be her legacy to me and my sister, if we could decode them and accept them.

And since I turned my back and walked to the car and returned to my life, I have not stopped scanning the horizon, seeking where to go next, where I could take my boys to find her and me and themselves. We will do what she did best, before we join her wherever she has gone to now.

97 Make a family cookbook

Grace, 39, Woodland Hills, CA

One Thanksgiving night, after my guests had left, I was watching a cooking show where the host's grandmother was teaching him how to make biscuits from a recipe given to her by her mother. I started to think about the good food that my family has made over the years and how I would like to have a collection of those recipes.

I composed a letter that night and asked my family, my husband's family, my sister's husband's family, etc., to send recipes, memories, and photographs that they, as a family, had shared during holidays, special occasions, and everyday meals. I wanted to collect favorite recipes from all members of the family — great-grandparents, grandparents, aunts, uncles, cousins, nephews, nieces, kids, and all extended family members — whoever liked to cook.

Specifically, I asked for original recipe cards from everyone and scanned those in so I would have everyone's original writing. I thought it would bring back memories to those who recognized their grandmother's writing from letters.

It took me a year to finish the project. I printed 250 copies. To represent the different cultures in our family — Jewish, Middle Eastern, Polish, and Italian — I named the cookbook *Blintzes and Baklava.*

Arranging the recipes in the traditional cookbook order — appetizers, side dishes, breads, main dishes, desserts — I also included an index in the back with everyone's name in alphabetical order, referencing their relation to the family and their recipe listed with a page number. It's a wonderfully diverse collection of recipes, like Grandma Gold's Excellent Challah, Mouloukhia (Egyptian Rice and Spinach), and Hungarian Torte. It's a collection of recipes, stories, and photographs that we can now pass down to future generations.

Be around to see my great-grandchildren - Visit the Vietnam memorial

Looking for something to pass on to those you leave behind?

A powerful way to impart cobbled advice and outdated preconceptions?

Capture your thoughts, fears, hopes, and beliefs for future generations to enjoy with a personal recording on video- or audiotape.

Turning 30?
Getting married?
Expecting a child?

Mark an occasion in your own life by recording something for a special event in someone else's.

Include *such intriguing information as:*

- Things you currently believe in.

- Proud achievements that history may forget.

- Dirty secrets that can only be revealed at a lifetime's distance.

Build something that lasts
John, 28, Amsterdam

I was given a pickax and a pair of goggles to protect my eyes from splinters of flying stone. In order to prove that I was not "soft," I immediately swung into action. I lunged at the rock like a maniac, until my fifth strike caused a shard of stone to leave a small crack in the window of the downstairs toilet. Jeff was delighted.

Although I had spent most weekends working on the family farm during my early to mid-teens, I had since tried to avoid the place. My Uncle Alan and his middle-aged workman, Jeff, had quietly frowned upon my decision not to leave school at the age of sixteen and come to work on the farm. Although this had not really soured our relationship, as they had put it down to "a phase I was going through," my subsequent decision to study medieval poetry at university had been met with outright disapproval, bordering on disgust.

When we were alone together, Jeff and I got on well, but in the presence of others he reveled in drawing attention to the contrast between the level of my college education and my lack of common sense. His most successful formula involved asking others if they thought I was capable of performing a simple task, while referring to me as either "Brains" or "Einstein." For example, he would nod in my direction and say to Uncle Alan something like, "I wonder if Einstein here knows how to use a tap." Or: "Do you think Brains here knows how a bucket works?" This became quite irritating.

Going to the farm as an unemployed undergraduate would be like stepping into hell. But — torn between this humiliation and the potentially greater humiliation of having to scrounge yet more cash from my dad while I searched for work — I went back to the farm.

> "Do you think Brains here knows how a bucket works?"

It being late winter, just before the lambing season, there wasn't really that much that needed to be done. Uncle Alan had an idea. There was a small parking area directly above the farmhouse, on slightly higher ground, where it was possible to park four vehicles. Carving a series of steps into a bank of rock behind the farmhouse would allow people to walk directly from the kitchen door to this parking area. I found the project rather daunting, as the stone looked quite hard, but, desperate to shed my reputation for being a "nancy boy," I managed to feign enthusiasm.

Those first few days were the hardest. Sometimes the pickax hit the rock with a heavy thud that seemed to bounce right back into my kidneys. But within a week, something resembling a series of eight steps had begun to emerge.

I became obsessed with making the steps perfect. The men would come back from the fields to find me crawling on my hands and knees with a ruler and spirit level, scratching at the rock with a small file while gently blowing away the resulting dust. After a total of three weeks, the job was finished. I had found the work really heavy. Some of my fingernails were broken and the skin on my hands was dry and cracked. But everyone agreed that I had done an excellent job.

Later that year, I went back to the farm to help bring in the hay. I no longer felt anxious about going there. Uncle Alan, Jeff, and I spent the day loading bales of hay onto a trailer, and then unloading them into a barn on the far side of the farm. By the time we had finished, we were thirsty and exhausted. Jeff drove the tractor back to the farmyard and the rest of us sat at the very back of the trailer, letting our legs dangle over the edge.

We sat in the sun for a while, drinking our beers. By the time I had finished my second can, I was feeling unusually happy and relaxed, and went to fetch more beer. Coming back from the house, via my recently created steps, I gazed down and experienced a sudden, unexpected flush of pride. The steps were incredibly robust, almost indestructible, and the thought flashed through my mind that they would most likely still be there long after me. I was thrilled to realize that I was capable of leaving some kind of indelible physical mark on the world. In a moment of booze-fueled recklessness, I decided to share these thoughts with the others.

After I had spoken, there followed a short, slightly uncomfortable silence. Then Jeff said, "Sounds like old Brainstein here's had a few too many."

Start all over again

Margaret, 27, Washington, DC

I've daydreamed for years about just starting over. About leaving everything behind and reinventing myself.

I don't want to be a quitter but there is a fine line between that and having the courage to make the right decision. Like in the movie *The Jerk*, I wanted to say, "All I need is this thermos." No job. No apartment. No big savings. No school. No boyfriend. No "perfect" plan.

So a few days before my 27th birthday, I bought a one-way flight to San Francisco from Washington, DC. I called work and quit. I wasn't depressed. I wasn't angry with my past. I love my family and I have tremendous friends. I just wanted to see if I could do it — prove to myself that I was capable of change.

I gave away most of my possessions and put a few irreplaceable items in a storage unit. I spent a quality weekend with my dad and had a summer BBQ with friends.

I'm flying over Pittsburgh as I write this. I expect there'll be literal and metaphorical turbulence, but I think I am going to be just fine.

Do or Die

"The left, logical side of the brain said, 'Don't be a dope, fatty, tell them the truth: You are afraid...'

"But the other side of my brain, the right side, the stupid side, the side that told me to become a journalist, and buy a pickup truck and grow a beard, said, 'Do it! You only live once!'"

Jim, #38 — *"Travel at the speed of sound"*

Everything starts with an idea.

Whether it's a secret desire to motorcycle across Canada, run a restaurant on the southwest coast of France, or start a charity that finds shelter for the homeless, or just a longing to learn the banjo, most of us could live all day in our imagination... It's a shame we have to come home.

So how do we make our ideas real?

The movies do it so much better — swirling clocks and calendar pages flipping away to illustrate the time passing. They skip past all the hard work, the early mornings, late nights, cold dinners, rejection letters, and unpaid bills. In the real world, there's a sorry lack of jump cuts or even a jaunty musical montage to help things along.

Given this, it's only natural to hold back and wait for the stars to align before taking our first steps. We all do this. It's hard not to. Avoiding the proverbial "blank page" is one of the top reasons why dishes get washed, desks cleared, and dogs walked. But every so often, for the ideas that genuinely matter to us, the curiosity to see what's around the corner will be matched by our resolve to see them through.

The 2DO List is a means of identifying those particular experiences we're really ready to work for. While you might choose to slip it in a drawer, or to bury it in the garden for future generations to discover, you might instead recognize in your choices a genuine call to action.

Few of us are going to pursue everything we've written down. Sometimes we're just going to want to take the day off, lie on the couch, and listen to the hum of the radiator. In fact, you may find that you can live a good life without doing 90% of your goals. If that's the case, it'll make it much easier to focus on the most important ones.

In the cold light of day, you might notice a number of ideas no longer seem so attractive ("own a chimpanzee," "start a detective agency" — what was I thinking?!). But before completely dismissing them, consider whether they've lost their appeal because they really are ridiculous, or because you're afraid they sound uncharacteristic or too difficult.

That said, not everything is going to require an epic struggle or involve a huge emotional investment. Always wanted to smoke a pipe? Wear a wig for a day? Cook a feast for friends? You could knock those three off by midnight (you might want to warn your friends about the wig, though...).

The following question game is there to help get you started in exploring the choices you make for your list. You don't have to rank your goals in any order, but it's useful to get a general sense of their size and shape. Having all the information about a particular goal can only take us so far. Recognizing why we wrote it down in the first place and knowing what we expect to get out of it can make even the most ambitious goals feel more manageable.

Look for common themes and motivations behind the goals and consider how the pieces fit together. You might find your 2DO List isn't as random as it first appears.

WHAT'S ON
**TAKE A
FRESH LOOK**
YOUR LIST?

Name a goal you could do today.

What three goals were you most surprised you wrote down?

Name a goal that would require you to pick up some new skills.

If you could do only five things on your list, which would they be?

Which goals would you most like to do with your partner or a friend?

Name three goals that could have the most positive impact on other people.

Place your bets...
Which of your goals really spark your imagination?
Which ones do you want to know more about?
Which ones can you live *without*?

77 65 12 87 5 33 92 31 50 26 15 4 61 24 41 36 89 10 53

What's your most challenging goal?

Name one goal you would want to keep a secret.

Name an ambitious goal you're willing to make sacrifices for.

Which is your most expensive goal to undertake? Your cheapest?

Name a goal that sounds good, but you don't actually expect to ever do.

Which of the ten story sections inspired the most of your goals? Which the least?

In the end...

Ambitious goals are always going to be hard to pull off. That's part of their attraction. They'll demand dedication and resourcefulness we didn't know we had. But the great satisfaction of turning an idea into reality — of turning nothing into something — can last a lifetime.

Nothing happens overnight. Steve Jobs started Apple Computers in his bedroom. Joseph Heller wrote *Catch-22* over eight years in the mornings before work. Anita Roddick first struggled through running a bed and breakfast before starting The Body Shop without anything close to a five-year plan. And there was no "alternative music" scene in the U.S. until the band Black Flag created a new network in the 1980s by sleeping on friends' couches and performing in people's living rooms.

It's not just the goals themselves that make the experience worthwhile. It's the mad pursuit of them that often resonates over time. Ambitions are unpredictable. Surprises and tangents will pepper the best-laid plans. Those discoveries along the way that we'd otherwise miss are what really make the trip worth taking.

And, of course, as we change, so will our lists. A few months from now, some of us will review what we've written down and find that some goals might require some serious editing (maybe it's not the house in Spain you're after as much as a fine patch of sun, a plate of *boquerones,* and the occasional bottle of Rioja...). Other ideas will still ring true, maybe even louder than before. By revisiting our 2DO List every once in a while, we can get a better sense of how far we've come and where we plan to go.

In the end, what constitutes a "life well-lived" is up to the individual. Looking back, it may be the small moments we remember most of all, along with the days spent with our friends, the things we built with our own hands, and the times we surprised ourselves by pushing harder than we previously thought possible.

There will always be some regret. We are always going to want a little more time, we are always going to wish for one more day. But, of course, it's not ours to demand. Knowing this, we can only do what any rational mind would do in this situation: enjoy it while we can.

T H E

2 DO

LIST

1
2
3
4
5
6
7
8
9
10
11
12
13
14
15
16
17
18
19
20
21
22
23
24
25

26
27
28
29
30
31
32
33
34
35
36
37
38
39
40
41
42
43
44
45
46
47
48
49
50

51
52
53
54
55
56
57
58
59
60
61
62
63
64
65
66
67
68
69
70
71
72
73
74
75

76	
77	
78	
79	
80	
81	
82	
83	
84	
85	
86	
87	
88	
89	
90	
91	
92	
93	
94	
95	
96	
97	
98	
99	
100	

Two heads really **are** better than one!!

Temper your pipe-dream with an injection of reality!

Why go it alone, when you can share the ride with a good friend? Discover which goal **they** would start with. Ask for advice, contacts, encouragement.

Nothing cuts through small-talk & straight to people's deepest ambitions quite like the 2DO List.

Why not share *yours* with someone today?

Dampen your defeatism with someone else's words of support!

Our Thanks

One of the great rewards these past couple of years working on 2DO has been the people we've met and talked with along the way. This particular "do or die" project would remain the stuff of barroom chitchat if it weren't for the immense generosity, encouragement, and expertise of many people. In particular, we would like to thank the following for putting us up, putting up with us, and pushing us further:

Ron Lieber and Jodi Kantor, Paul Mahon, Daniel Greenberg, Jane Ottenberg, Jo Roeber, Martin Rosendaal, Sophie Spencer-Wood, Michael Hunt, Peter Dean, Adam Oliver, Harry Hobson, Mike Anderson, Matt Brown, Margaret Ogden, Olly Montagu, Justin Hall, Peter Georgescu, Jef Mcallister, Adam and Shana Suschitzsky, Ioannis Iordanidis, Fiona Mayfield, Franklin Adams, Liz Matthews, John Forsyth, Burke Berendes, Greg Sinden, Peter Pelham, and Chris Banks. Our great thanks too to the team at Little, Brown and Company, especially Terry Adams, Sarah Brennan, Marie Mundaca, and Claire Smith. And finally we are forever grateful to our families, in particular to our partners, Victoria and Vicki, whose love, support, patience, and good humor made this book possible.

A special thanks to everyone who has taken the time to share their stories, particularly those whose submissions are included in this book:

Sharon R. Amos, Susie Anderson, Shaun Askew, Kevin Asseo, Alice Barclay, Zina Baumann, Margaret Bennett, Matt Berendes, Paul Bloom, Eric Brach, Matt Brown, Bruce Campbell, Emanuel Carpenter, Andrew Choate, James Clarke, SuzAnne C. Cole, Colin Day, Sarah DeBacher, Daniel Degnan, Elizabeth Dunning, Page Evans, Kate Ferguson, Hana S. Field, Julianne Flynn, Chris Friendly, Graham Gardner, Richard Goldstein, Thelma Goldstein, Eric Halvorson, Harry Hobson, Celine Hollinshead, Amy Hsu, James O. Jackson, Leslie Jolly, Nic Kelman, Grace Beth Kilzi, Laurie Little, Sandy MacDonald, Eric Mahoney, Diana May, Michael Meyerhofer, Johanna Miflin, Olly Montagu, Moshe Morris, Daniel Mudford, Andy Myers, Eric Myers, Karen Myers, Ana Maria Nezol, Chris Ogden, Hun Ohm, Miriam Parker, Christopher Petty, John Powell, Jennifer Robinson, Dorothy Robinson, Chad Ruble, Mary Schodorf, Mandy Settembre, Peter J. Shaw, David Henry Sterry, Tom Stokes, Neil Taplin, Tim Thornton, Benjamin Wagner, Pete Woodhead, Caitlin Zaloom, Sherryl Zounes.

Olly Montagu

Raised in Chicago and Washington DC, Michael Ogden (left) is a 33-year-old writer, editor, and producer currently living in London. Highlights from his own list of things to do involve hopping a train from Moscow to St. Petersburg, getting married, and playing at an open mic night in his grandfather's pinstripe suit.

Chris Day (right) is a 30-year-old illustrator living in London. His 2DO List included giving a speech, smoking a pipe, and starting a family. As such, he has recently enjoyed many a winter's eve puffing smoke rings and passing on the skills of oration to his newborn son.

This is their first book. For more details, and more stories, please visit www.2dobeforeidie.com.